THE INVISIBLE BOND

How to Break Free from Your Sexual Past

Barbara Wilson

Multnomah® Publishers *Sisters, Oregon*

THE INVISIBLE BOND
published by Multnomah Publishers, Inc.
© 2006 by Barbara Wilson
International Standard Book Number: 1-59052-542-6

Cover design by Studiogearbox.com
Interior design and typeset by Katherine Lloyd, The DESK

Unless other indicated, Scripture quotations are from:
The Holy Bible, New International Version
©1973, 1978, 1984 by International Bible Society.
Used by permission of Zondervan Publishing House

Other Scripture quotations are from:
The Holy Bible, New King James Version (NKJV)
© 1984 by Thomas Nelson, Inc.
The Holy Bible, King James Version (KJV)
New American Standard Bible® (NASB) © 1960, 1977, 1995 by the
Lockman Foundation. Used by permission.

Some details in this book (including names of people,
cities, and businesses) have been changed.

Multnomah is a trademark of Multnomah Publishers, Inc.,
and is registered in the U.S. Patent and Trademark Office.
The colophon is a trademark of Multnomah Publishers, Inc.
Printed in the United States of America

For information:
MULTNOMAH PUBLISHERS, INC.
601 N LARCH STREET • SISTERS, OREGON 97759

Library of Congress Cataloging-in-Publication Data
Wilson, Barbara (Barbara T.)
The invisible bond / Barbara Wilson.
      p. cm.
Includes bibliographical references.
ISBN 1-59052-542-6
1. Lust--Religious aspects--Christianity. 2. Sex--Religious aspects--
Christianity. I. Title.
BV4627.L8W55 2006
241'.66--dc22   2005030233
         06 07 08 09 10 11 12 — 10 9 8 7 6 5 4 3 2 1 0

Contents

To my best friend on earth,
This was your dream for me.
Thank you for always trusting,
always hoping, and always persevering.
I will always love you.

To my best Friend in heaven,
This is Your story, You are the Star.
I will sing Your praises forever and ever.

Foreword

I n a world rampant with pornography, affairs, and sexual abuse, there are many wounded hearts. It would be so wonderful if these wounds would heal with the passing of time. Sadly, rather than time healing wounds, it seems to infect and magnify them. Those who have been hurt find many difficult and different ways to cope and survive. At best, life becomes a fight for acceptance, love, and a belief that one day it will all be better.

Fortunately, one day it can be better, but it will require some choices to promote healing. Waiting for God to do what God is waiting for us to do only creates false hopes and unrealistic expectations. There has to be a plan. There must be a path toward healing the wounds and building a fulfilling life rich with loving relationships.

Choosing to read *The Invisible Bond* could be the most significant decision you have made. The path to healing is in here. The path, plus time, plus your healing choices, can lead to healing and healthy connections with others.

I commend you for taking the journey to repair your heart. Know that God loves you and is there for you as you discover His truth and implement it into your life.

—Stephen Arterburn, founder
New Life Ministries

THE INFLUENCE
OF THE INVISIBLE

What do you know? Another book on sex.

There are so many. How to have sex. How to have great sex. God's view of sex. The world's view of sex. Help for those addicted to sex or pornography. And probably the greatest need for youth and singles...how *not* to have sex before you're married.

But this book is different. We're not going to talk about you having sex, but about *sex having you*. Sex is like superglue for humans. It creates incredibly powerful bonds—invisible bonds—between the bodies, souls, minds, and spirits of a man and a woman. And that's the way God intentionally designed us—to become sexually bonded for life with one marriage partner. It's one of His most amazing gifts to us.

But the gift becomes a liability for humans who have multiple sexual partners.

Sexual "Fine Print"

"What's the big deal?" you may be asking. "It's only sex. How does switching partners have any lasting effect on my mind, body, soul, or spirit?"

Or perhaps you're married now and your past sexual relationships are just that…past. Done. Out of sight and out of mind. You've admitted they were wrong, and you've asked God for forgiveness. Case closed. How can they impact you now?

God says in His Word that when we engage in the intimate act of sexual relations with someone, we become *one* with that person. We enter into an all-encompassing union involving our immaterial components, as well as our bodies.

What happens, then, when I become one with multiple partners? On the surface, my body, as well as my conscious affection and attention, may move on to someone new after a breakup. But what about my soul, my spirit, my mind? Are they able to put the past behind so easily? Can every part of me move into the next relationship unaffected, with no lingering residue from the previous ones? If there is sexual residue, what does it consist of? How does it impact me now or in future relationships?

I travel the country communicating on this topic, and most people I've met have a sexual past. The sexual revolution promised fun, excitement, intimacy, and love, but delivered pain, emptiness, divorce, disease, and death instead. Forty-plus years of sexual promiscuity have yielded a harvest of wounded, broken men and women.

How has your sexual past affected you? I'm going to help you begin answering that question right now. Start out with this exercise: Take a moment and think back to your

very first sexual experience, and then consider later stages
of your sexual history. Ask God to help you remember some
of the details, especially if you've buried them deep because
of pain or shame.

- Were you married or single? An adult, teen, or
  child?
- Were you in a serious relationship, or was it a
  one-night stand?
- Was it consensual, or were you a victim?
- Was your first experience a case of sexual abuse
  as a child? Did you become sexually promiscuous
  as a teen or young adult?
- If you were involved in a relationship, would
  you characterize it as positive or negative?
- How painful was the break-up for you?
- After you broke up, how soon did you initiate
  sex in your next relationship?
- If you waited for marriage to have sex, but then
  later divorced, did you became promiscuous
  prior to your second marriage?
- How many sexual partners have you had?
- If you had a third relationship, or a fourth—or
  any number—think about the circumstances of
  each one.
- You may be in a committed, loving marriage
  relationship right now, but when you make love
  do the faces of past lovers sometimes flash
  through your mind? Do you find yourself com-
  paring your spouse's lovemaking abilities with
  others from the past?

- Do you often find yourself fantasizing about past lovers: *What if I had married him or her instead?*
- Have you married for a second or third time only to find history repeating itself? *What is wrong with me?* you ask. *Why can't I pick the right one?*
- Did you enjoy sex before you were married, but now it's not so exciting? Or do you have to conjure up pornographic images to become aroused during lovemaking?
- Do you find that even though you're married you can't resist flirting with members of the opposite sex and desiring their attention?
- Do you experience shame and regret when you think about your past sexual relationships? Are you afraid that someone will find out?
- Do you struggle with trust, faithfulness, commitment, and emotional intimacy in relationships?

This is a long list, but it is by no means exhaustive. Did you see yourself in it? Can you relate to any of these questions and scenarios?

To help you further understand the impact of your sexual past, I've provided two "Symptom Checklists" in the appendix of this book. I'll discuss these in greater detail in chapter 7, but please take a few minutes now and complete the first checklist. Mark your scores for both the past and the present in the two columns on the right side of the checklist.

Once you have finished, scan back over your responses. What do your answers reveal about the physical and emotional symptoms that sexual residue has manifested in your past? How is it affecting you in the present?

Later, after you've finished working through this book and the first part of God's healing journey for you, I'll ask you to complete the second checklist. This will provide you with measurable proof of God's healing work in your life.

Invisible, but Not Inconsequential

So why make so much noise about sexual bonding? Why can't we simply leave the past behind?

That would be precisely the strategy I would recommend if not for the fact that these invisible bonds from the past continue to exercise profound influence in the present. Sexual bonding has the potential to radically alter your view of yourself, of others, and of sex. It can propel you along a destructive course of promiscuity and other high-risk behaviors. It can impair your ability to choose healthy people to date and marry. It can lead to sexual addiction or sexual dysfunction. And it can affect your ability to have close, intimate relationships with others and with God.

Inside marriage, God designed sex to be a bond that is powerful and unifying. Outside marriage, the bonds of sex can be devastating. Long after the lover has gone, the bond we've created stays with us, impacting our lives and future relationships in a negative way.

Research shows that teenagers who initiated sexual activity at a young age and have had multiple partners are less than half as likely to have stable, committed relationships in their thirties, when compared with those who waited to initiate sex later in life.[1] The greater the number of sexual partners, the greater the harmful residue, and the greater the long-term impact.

If you find these words speaking to you, you're not alone. As I speak to teens and young adults, and as I work closely with hurting men and women, I hear the same stories thousands of times over. There isn't anything you could tell me right now that I haven't heard from countless others. One after the other, in hesitant, broken words laden with shame and fear, people recount to me their sad, hidden secrets. I hear it all—more than I could ever have imagined.

And God hears it, too. He hears all the anguished cries of hurting people like you. He empathizes with your pain and struggles. He sees your broken heart, He feels your wounds, and He knows the rocky path you walk every day.

Not only does God hear, but He also offers hope, help, and answers. His heart breaks with yours, and He holds out hands of love, grace, mercy, forgiveness, healing, peace, rest, joy, and compassion. He promises to renew, restore, rebuild, and reward.

He's done it for me. For years I tried fixing myself, but nothing worked. God is the only One who could provide what I desperately needed. God performed a miracle of forgiveness and healing. He broke the sexual bonds that were destroying my life.

No physical healing I've ever experienced can compare to the marvel of God's grace in my life. Before He stepped in, the memories from years past loomed large, as though they had happened yesterday. Shame crashed down on me and engulfed me like a wave. But now the memories have faded into the distance.

The greatest miracle of all is the absence of shame. For the first time in twenty-five years, I no longer find my identity in what I did, but in what God has done in and for me.

Many others have taken this journey with God and have been freed from their invisible bonds. Vicki is one of those who discovered the power of God's forgiveness and healing from a promiscuous past. "Even after I had been a Christian for several years, my ministry and relationships seemed to keep running into a wall. How can you serve freely when chained to the guilt of a sexual past and blinded by selfishness? God took me on a journey, washing me with His forgiveness and then healing my wounds with His blood. Today I serve Him with a clear conscience in liberty and joy. I am a victorious new woman—His healing has changed my life."

I found Bruce's story fascinating. Because of his sexual bonding, he became addicted to the sport of sexual conquest. "A good day," he said, "whether married or single, revolved around having sex." He now sees that this was sex without intimacy, relationship, and trust. In the process he became desensitized to the seriousness of what he was doing and came to view women as sexual objects. When God began to work in Bruce's life, he decided to pursue purity in his dating relationships. "This changed my focus," he told me. "Before, promiscuity rated higher than compatibility in choosing a date. Now I avoid promiscuous women and am genuinely interested in getting to know women as people. My sexual healing has been a release from the worship of flesh, freeing me for the rightful worship of my Savior."

Shedding Light on the Unseen

Yes, this is another book on sex. But it's also much more. It's a book about breaking invisible, destructive bonds. It's a story of redemption. It's a message of hope and love from an amazing God who has a purpose for your life. It's a promise of healing and wholeness so you can experience all that God has to offer. It's a chance to hear a voice of truth about yourself and about sex, instead of the other voices you've been listening to.

Can you relate to what you've read so far? Can you see yourself in any of my questions or in these people's stories? Then I urge you to listen to your heart and say yes to all God has waiting for you. I invite you to turn the page and take this incredible journey with me.

As you break free from the weight of your past, prepare to soar.

Part One

A HEART IN **BONDAGE**

A HEART IN BONDAGE A HEART IN BONDAGE A HEART IN BONDAGE A HEART IN BONDAGE A HEART IN BONDAGE A HEART IN BONDAGE A HEART IN BONDAGE A HEART IN BONDAGE

Chapter One

DIARY OF A BONDED HEART

My Story

Everyone has a story. I never knew that. I thought I was the only one. For twenty-five years I never told anyone my story, and no one told me theirs.

No one else could be this sinful, I told myself. Especially not my Christian friends.

Week in and week out, I served in church with these dear friends, prayed with them, socialized with them, and even shared burdens with them in small groups. But no one told me their secrets. So there weren't any, right?

Wrong. Everyone has a story. But no one is telling it.

That all changed when I began to tell my story. Suddenly everyone was revealing their secrets with me—tales that made mine seem less traumatic in comparison. I was amazed.

What keeps us silent? I began to wonder. Why can't we be honest? And why now, when I open up, do others feel comfortable doing the same?

I've discovered that keeping secrets is Satan's idea, and being open and honest is God's. Doing it Satan's way means wearing a mask every day, everywhere. God's way means we can be real, open, and honest. All the time. Keeping secrets isolates us from God and others and leaves us at the mercy of Satan's condemnation, which further seals our silence, convincing us that we must never share our secret.

Telling our stories breaks the grip of the secret, diffusing its power. Exposing the secret makes it shrink, while hiding it allows it to grow bigger and uglier. Keeping silent means we bear the load alone. Opening up allows others to share our burden, our pain, our shame. Silence inhibits healing; openness facilitates it.

Every time someone shares their secret with me, I can't help becoming excited for them, because I know they are taking the first step towards healing. Not only do I have the awesome privilege of offering God's grace and compassion—as others did for me—but I get to relieve them of some of their burden.

Patty wanted to meet me out on the dark, cold patio. It was 10 p.m., and she had waited for over an hour. She was about to share something with me that no one else knew.

She could hardly look me in the eye. As I held her hand, she told me a gruesome story of pornography and homosexual experimenting, all while she was married. At first she was hesitant, but I saw her hope and confidence grow as she realized that I was going to accept her anyway, even when I had heard the worst. She hadn't intended to tell me everything—just the vague basics. But God's grace through me gave her the courage to get it all out—every last, ugly detail.

By the time we were finished talking and praying two

hours later, Patty had changed. She still had problems and a lot of work to do before she'd be free of her invisible bonds. But her countenance had changed. She looked more relaxed, more at peace, and more hopeful. God had taken some of her burden and taken it on Himself, and for the first time in many years, Patty knew she wasn't alone. She had finally discovered hope of forgiveness and healing.

Patty took the first step towards healing when she yielded to God's Spirit, urging her to tell someone.

It wasn't very long ago that I took that same step. And as God promised, He's proven faithful, working out complete healing in my life.

You have a story. Maybe no one knows what it is, because you haven't told it. The fact that you're reading this book means that God has been tugging at your heart.

I'm excited for you. You're about to take the first step towards something wonderful, something miraculous—the burden-lifting, secret-shrinking, healing grace of God.

A Series of Unintended Events

I never planned for any of it to happen. Not like this. And certainly not with him.

That was my problem right there—I didn't plan. I've since heard that great line: "No one plans to fail; they fail to plan." I can't think of a better description for my life.

I was raised in a Christian home in Canada, with a stay-at-home mom and a Baptist pastor father. When I was seven, I gave my heart to Jesus and began an incredible walk with Him. As early as fourth and fifth grade, I began to share my faith openly. I conspicuously brought my Bible to school and kept it on my desk. In high school, I started a student Bible study, and at fifteen began my public speaking experience at a Christian summer camp. My relationship with God was everything to me.

Then one day I chose to walk away from God.

I didn't mean to. I wasn't even aware that I was doing it.

In the fall of 1974 my parents planned to send my brother to a Christian high school two provinces away. (Provinces are the "states" of Canada.) It sounded like a fun adventure, an opportunity to see beyond my tiny town—population two hundred. I asked if I could go, too. My parents agreed. And so off I went, full of enthusiasm and hope.

Ignorant of the consequences, I began to make some choices that determined the direction of my life for the next several years. I'm still not sure how it happened, but the love and desire of my life was directed away from God and toward a handsome young man. We met at a Christian school, so in my clouded thinking I assumed he was God's choice for me. I gave up everything for this man's love: my virginity, my family, my home, my faith, and my morals. I began to travel down a road that I had never imagined possible—a road that would take me to the bottom.

After graduation, against my parents' wishes, I ran away to be with my boyfriend. At first we lived together, and then at the tender age of eighteen, we secretly tied the knot in a little wedding chapel across the border in Idaho. As the months went on, I began to regret what I had done and knew that I had made a terrible mistake. So two years later, a humbled and broken young woman found her way back home. I was filled with regret for the pain I had caused my parents, and shame for how my misguided relationship had started. Under this unrelenting emotional burden, I bought into the enemy's lie that I had already traveled too far down this road to turn back. It was too late. No one, I thought, would accept me now.

I wasn't expecting to feel so alone and empty after leaving my husband. But rather than going to God—the *only* One who could fulfill my need for love and intimacy—I began to live a dual life. I lived one existence during the week and another on Sunday. Six days a week, I tried to satisfy my relational hunger in the arms of other men. I was oblivious to the danger of my actions until the day I heard the words, "You're pregnant."

A truckload of emotions slammed into me—fear, disbelief, regret, denial. I could not have this baby. First of all, I was a preacher's kid, accountable to a higher set of standards than others. And I was still married, caught in a divorce process that would take three years.

I had already broken my parents' hearts once. If they discovered my pregnancy, it would devastate them all over again. So it was "the pregnancy" that had to go.

After all, I reasoned half-heartedly, it's only a blob of tissue. Right?

Right?

Isn't that what everyone said? Who was I to argue with the experts?

So, one cold January day I had an abortion.

I put to death two people that day—my daughter and myself. She was ushered into the presence of God, while I sentenced myself to the deepest, darkest prison. There, every moment for the next twenty-five years, I tortured myself in payment for my crime.

I could go no lower. In my opinion there was nothing

worse than taking someone's life. I, a girl born in a Christian family and raised according to Christian values, had just committed *murder.*

Prison Life

Over and over in His Word, God has warned us not to have sex outside of marriage. *What is the big deal?* I used to think.

Now I knew the answer from firsthand experience, and I wished I could take it all back. Hindsight is painful. And so is the futile speculation on what might have been. *What have I given up by being so reckless and self-centered? Where might I be now if I had followed God's direction for my life?*

But the scariest thought of all was that God would never be able to use me…someone so sinful, so stained, so full of shame.

Looking back at the young, innocent girl I had been, heading off for a fantastic adventure, I could see that I had left my guard down. Without the supervision of my parents, the accountability of my small group, or the biblical teaching from my youth pastor, I was like a lamb trotting gleefully into a pack of wolves. The wolves caught me off guard.

I hadn't planned to meet someone. I hadn't planned a strategy regarding sex before marriage. I hadn't planned to fail. I failed to plan.

I was young and immature, unaware that there was a real enemy, and oblivious that he was calling my name. Sometimes the enemy can be so attractive. But looking back, his strategy was obvious: I was young and far from home, hungry for friends, with easy, unsupervised access to my boyfriend all day, every day. Add to that the illusion of head-over-heels love with the man I was convinced was *the one.*

And there I was. Vulnerable. An easy target.

It's not as though God wasn't trying to get through to me. He was, loud and clear. But I had turned down the volume on my spiritual radio. Each time I ignored Him, my heart grew a little harder. I rationalized that I had chosen a great "Christian" guy, and we were at a Christian school. This had to be heaven-sent, divinely sanctioned.

Didn't it?

I've since learned that when we turn the volume down—when we harden our hearts to God's voice—we are capable of *anything*. I'm humbled to say that I proved that shameful truth myself.

Solitary Confinement

Eventually, four years after coming home, I met and married a wonderful man, had four children, and began a new life.

But I lived perpetually in my self-made prison of pain and shame. Every day I exacted a price from myself in payment for my sins. My punishment took on many forms, all fueled by this one thought: *I will never again be good enough.* I was shackled by a constant striving to do and be whatever it might take to feel good enough.

As a prisoner, I became shy and defensive against perceived unjust accusations. I frequently lashed out at my family and friends. To compensate for my lack of self-worth, I put on an air of self-sufficient confidence and perfection. To keep anyone from figuring out my strategy—because then I'd have to reveal the truth—I closed myself off from my husband and friends.

Just last year God showed me that I have never truly been close and intimate with *anyone*. I had so isolated myself that I didn't even know my own feelings. I became judgmental and adopted unrealistic expectations of others. And I suffered from anxiety and depression.

As a mom, I was overprotective and controlling. I was afraid of two things: that my kids would one day find out about my past and that they might then follow in my footsteps. In fact, I was so afraid of being found out that I spent my life constantly hiding, protecting myself. My paranoia sucked the life out of me and everyone close to me.

It was a horrible way to live, and yet I became used to it. When I managed to back far enough into denial, my life actually seemed enjoyable. No one looking at me knew the intense struggle going on inside. I was an expert at accessorizing—choosing the perfect mask for each social occasion. The irony was that I felt I needed to do this so that people would like and accept me. But instead I intimidated them and kept them at arm's length. It was a vicious cycle. And it wasn't working.

In Isaiah 61:1, the Messiah says, "He has sent me to bind up the brokenhearted, to proclaim freedom for the captives and release from darkness for the prisoners." The Hebrew word for "the prisoners" can be literally translated "the blind." The blind don't know it's dark because they can't see. This was me—living in the hell of darkness, but not even aware of it.

I had asked God to forgive me several times. I knew then as I know now that when we ask for forgiveness, God forgives. So why didn't I *feel* forgiven? Why couldn't I forgive myself? Why, whenever I thought about my past, was I overcome with shame…the worst kind of shame…the kind that propels you further into the prison of emotional isolation and secrecy?

When I least expected it, with sudden force the shame would slam into me. I'd be listening to talk radio in the car and the topic would be abortion. But the story always went like this: "Yes, I had an abortion, but *then* I became a Christian." What I heard was, "A *real* Christian wouldn't find herself in this position." *Wham!*

I'd be having fun with friends, and someone would share the perfect story of saving herself sexually for marriage, meeting Mr. Right, and living happily ever after. No regrets. *Wham!*

I'd be sitting in an adult Sunday school class, watching a video on abortion, convincing myself that I could handle it this time. After all, it had been so long ago. But I always ran out sobbing. *Wham! Wham!*

Or worst of all, I'd be lying in bed at night, with the enemy whispering in my ear: *Look at your twins, born premature and disabled. It's entirely your fault!*

Wham! *Wham!* WHAM!

The Day the Sun Shone In

My story does have a good ending. A great ending, in fact.

I failed to plan. But God didn't. In His perfect time and in His perfect way, He interrupted me one day to redirect me toward a new, better plan for my life. I guess God knew I was stuck and needed a little push in His direction. So one day He moved our family from our home in Canada to California where we knew *no one.* Ouch! All I had was Him.

I love God's attention to detail. After twenty-five years, He took me 2,500 miles away to a place where He could get my attention. And He got it. I began a new relationship with God. In California, I couldn't rely on my old way of doing things—even with God. And so for the first time in my life, I began to slowly surrender everything to Him, allowing Him to thaw my frozen heart.

In Psalm 118:5, David says, "In my anguish I cried to the LORD, and he answered by setting me free." One day, from deep within my prison cell, I literally cried out to God in anguish. The first thing He did was shine His light into my dungeon. In that moment, I saw clearly the sad, dingy reality of my existence up to that point. I saw the truth. I had sentenced myself there for life, but God had come to set me free.

I'm so thankful He was there, listening for my feeble cry. He never gave up on me. He had waited for me to ask, waited for me to accept, not only His forgiveness, but His complete healing as well.

And wouldn't you know it? The first thing He made me face was my abortion. From there we dealt with the sexual promiscuity, the divorce…every last shameful bit of my prodigal detour.

It was time for healing. My journey to freedom was about to begin.

Hope for Anyone

What are you trying to hide? What secrets are locked away in your closet? Sexual promiscuity? Abortion? Abuse? Rape? Homosexuality? Addiction?

Did reading my story spark any painful emotions or memories? Were you able to relate to my prison, my pain, my shame?

Maybe you're wondering what a sexually bonded heart looks like and whether you have one. Maybe you're asking the heartfelt question I hear so often: "How can I break my sexual bonds?"

If so, then keep reading. I've got some great news just for you.

RECOGNIZING THE SEXUALLY BONDED HEART

What Is It? Do I Have One?

've done it a hundred times, and it never ceases to send a chill down my spine. This simple object lesson is the most graphic and sobering visual demonstration of sexually bonded hearts I've ever seen. It speaks a thousand words in one simple motion.

But for some reason, this time with these particular students, the imagery's vivid eloquence electrified the room with unusual intensity.

As an abstinence educator, I have the privilege of speaking to hundreds of high school and college students about why saving sex for marriage is one of the greatest decisions they can make for their future. I do the heart demonstration every time. But this group was different in many ways. They were college students, and they didn't *have* to be there. They came voluntarily to hear me share the incredible benefits God held in store for them if they would save sex for marriage. This was my second session with them, and there were significantly more young people in attendance tonight than the previous week. They came hungry—not for food, but for hope. I could see it. I could feel it. I could hear it. By the time I came to the heart demonstration, all of them were leaning forward with anticipation, straining for my next words.

I held up two differently colored construction-paper hearts, representing a girl (Jan) and a boy (Dan).

"Jan and Dan were in love," I began. "Even though they didn't really want to have sex, they hadn't made any previous decisions about sexual intimacy. They didn't set mutually agreed-upon boundaries. Their passion snuck up on them, they got carried away, and...*it* happened."

I stapled the two hearts together with a few staples.

Then I explained, "God says that when we have a sexual relationship with someone, the bonding is not just physical. It's emotional, spiritual, and mental as well. It is a complete and total union. God says we are no longer two, but one. Mark 10:7–8 says, 'For this reason a man will leave his father and mother and be united to his wife, and the two will become one flesh. So they are no longer two, but one.'

"However, it's not just the marriage relationship that creates this bonding. Having sex with anyone outside of marriage will create it as well. First Corinthians 6:16 says, 'Do you not know that he who unites himself with a prostitute is one with her in body? For it is said, "The two will become one flesh."'"

I glanced around the classroom. Several heads nodded.

I continued to explain that prostitution has been around since biblical times. Prostitutes offer sex, not marriage. The phrase "the two will become one flesh" means the same in both Mark 10:8 and 1 Corinthians 6:16—that is, both in the context of marriage and in a physical relationship with a prostitute. This complete and intense bonding happens in a sexual relationship whether you're married or not.

In his book *Restoring Sexual Sanity*, Randy Alcorn talks about how God designed the sexual union to be a truly intimate experience. The primary word used in the Old Testament for sexual intercourse is *yada*, which means "to know." Genesis 4:1 NKJV says, "Now Adam *knew* Eve his wife, and she conceived and bore Cain" (emphasis mine). The kind of intimacy characterized by yada is not a distant, merely factual knowledge, but a personal, intimate, and experiential knowledge one person has of another.

Yada is the same word that is used to describe a believer's relationship with his God (for example, Daniel 11:32, "the people who know [yada] their God"). Alcorn says, "To know one's marriage partner in the act of sex is analogous to developing intimacy with God."[1] In sexual intercourse, God has given us a living picture illustrating what it means to be one with Him. This is one reason that sex is holy.

Holy sex? Is that a new concept for you? It was for me. But then I realized that my view of sex and God's view of sex weren't the same. And God's view wasn't the one that needed to change. Our culture's understanding of sex has become so perverted that it's hard for us to imagine it being holy. But we return to the holiness of sex when we realize that God used it to shed light on the greatest intimate relationship ever known—our relationship with Him.

When you participate in a sexual relationship, whether you wait until you're married or not, your relationship with your partner changes. You have just possessed one another in the most intimate way humanly possible, and it impacts your entire being to the core—spiritually, emotionally, and mentally. If you save sex until you're married, it serves as the incredible expression of a love that has first grown and deepened through nonsexual means, by the cultivation of true intimacy in a friendship. You already *feel* close; now the sexual relationship enhances and deepens that closeness. This is holy sex.

But 1 Thessalonians 4:4–6 says, "Each of you should learn to control his own body in a way that is holy and honorable, not in passionate lust like the heathen, who do not know God; and that in this matter no one should wrong his brother or *take advantage* of him" (emphasis mine). The word for "take advantage" can also be translated "defraud." When we participate in sex outside of marriage, the Bible says we are defrauding each other. We're robbing or cheating each other by creating a desire that we cannot fulfill—the desire for commitment, security, and oneness that can only be found in marriage. When those desires are not fulfilled, the relationship will eventually end. A 1996 Gallup Poll[2] survey found that the number-one reason teen relationships break up is because the partners have had sex. If the desires for commitment created by the sex are not fulfilled, partners in the relationship can come to resent one another.

Right Desire, Wrong Path

That's exactly what happened to Jan and Dan.

In that crowded classroom, I continued their story. "Jan and Dan's love turned to resentment because they had prematurely created a union that they were not ready to commit to. So they broke up.

"But here's the painful irony. This bonding is so special and desirable that with each future relationship, Jan and Dan will be tempted to initiate a sexual union sooner and sooner to recreate this sense of closeness and intimacy, only to have it end in the same way."

Dr. Donald Joy, in his book *Re-bonding: Preventing and Restoring Damaged Relationships*,[3] suggests that because sexual intercourse is an intense bonding experience between two partners, it feeds a desire to repeat the act in order to feel nurtured again. When one illicit sexual relationship ends and another begins, the couple progresses rapidly to sexual intimacy in order to recreate the bonding they've come to expect.

What we are really looking for when having sex outside of marriage is true intimacy—interpersonal communication at the deepest level. We look to sex to provide the closeness and love that we're longing for.

The desire for intimacy is a pure and good desire, because it is planted within us by God. We have been created to desire, to desperately long for, intimacy with Him, and to enjoy the same sense of intimacy through marriage and married sex. But nonmarital sex has become a cheap imitation of true intimacy in our culture, and it has taken our focus off the only One who can ultimately satisfy our inner longings for love and intimacy. Sex makes us *feel* close even when we hardly know each other. Yet, couples who initiate sex early on in their relationship will have difficulty moving to that deepest level and experiencing true intimacy with each other. In a later chapter, we'll discuss why this happens.

The Injury You Didn't Know You Had

Finally, we had come to the most startling moment in my presentation. I held up the two hearts and, to signify Dan and Jan's breakup, I pulled them apart. My unsuspecting audience was shocked when they saw the result.

The hearts were not just stapled loosely, as they appeared to be. Previously, I had glued the hearts together. So instead of separating easily and intact, the hearts were literally torn apart—each leaving pieces behind, still attached to the other. Neither heart came away whole.

I had started with two individual hearts. But what I tore apart was a single, united whole.

The visual demonstration delivered its message effectively. In a thousand unspoken words, it made astonishingly visible and tangible the invisible reality of the sexually bonded heart. In the beginning there was hope of love and commitment, but in the end there was only brokenness and pain.

The room was suddenly very still. Every eye and ear was tuned in. My heart broke as I realized that they knew exactly what I was talking about. Not from reading about it or hearing about it from someone else. They had experienced it. The wreckage of the paper hearts reflected *their own* heartfelt pain.

The hidden tragedy of the invisible bond is that the wounded hearts, with parts of someone else attached to them, will next go off to create unions with yet more unsuspecting hearts, subjecting self and others repeatedly to this same inner mutilation. Even if your only experience of premarital sex was with your current spouse, you created a sexual bond with him or her that needs to be broken. Your premarital sexual involvement, though now out of sight and mind, is nonetheless negatively impacting your marriage today. You feel the consequences, but you probably don't understand the source.

I call this lingering residue "sexual baggage." Whether you participated voluntarily or involuntarily in premarital sex, invisible bonding has occurred, leaving behind damaged, wounded emotions. Sexual bonding is a lose-lose prospect outside of marriage. It hurts both participants.

Just Another Sin?

First Corinthians 6:18 says, "Flee from sexual immorality. All other sins a man commits are outside his body, but he who sins sexually sins against his own body." Sexual sin is not worse than other sins, but it is different. It's a sin that we commit against ourselves.

This verse never made sense to me before. How do we sin against ourselves? How does sexual sin hurt us? Or the other person, for that matter? Have you ever thought about that?

Our culture asks rationalizing questions like these all the time. *What is the fuss? It's only sex. It's not hurting anybody.*

That's the way Lindsay justified giving away her virginity while attending Bible college. But the consequences over the next several years would progressively and painfully unveil the significance of that one seemingly harmless action. Lindsay learned she was pregnant, and in order to hide her sexual sin, she had an abortion. She was horrified by what she had done, so she married the baby's father, hoping this would make up for all the wrong...might somehow make it right. She had bought into the enemy's lie that she had to *perform* in order to be acceptable to God. If she married the man, maybe God would not look so harshly on her sin.

The marriage ended up lasting for sixteen loveless and abusive years. After divorcing her husband, Lindsay proceeded on into two other sexually intimate relationships, each of which almost resulted in marriage. Lindsay gave a piece of herself away with each relationship and ended up emotionally empty and broken...filled with shame.

She really didn't want to do any of this. She knew all along that these actions were wrong.

Her efforts to earn her way into God's good graces by self-effort only caused further destruction. Destruction is usually the result when we behave according to the enemy's lies. I am not sure why we are so easily deceived by this one—the lie that we can work hard enough to make God accept us—but it's one I've believed myself.

During and after my moral slide, the fact that I was a Christian intensified my shame. For some reason, I had this self-righteous idea that, because I should've known better, I was more culpable. My sin seemed more horrendous, and therefore more unforgivable. I thought that it would be easier for God to forgive someone who wasn't aware of the Bible's teaching on sexual sin. So I, like Lindsay, set out on a life journey, trying to make all the wrongs right.

This is the dynamic by which Lindsay and I and so many other men and women have—through sex outside of marriage—sinned against our own bodies, as well as against our fragile, vulnerable inner being. These invisible bonds and the invisible wounds they leave behind are self-inflicted.

But sexual sin doesn't just wound the perpetrator. It also hurts everyone around us. Wherever we go, we can't avoid encounters with people—encounters in which others unwittingly prod our unseen, raw wounds. We react by defending, attacking, and withdrawing. Spouses, children, coworkers, friends—even the checker at the grocery store—can unknowingly say or do something that lances an inner injury, and pussy ugliness pours out.

Each wound caused by sexual bonding is as unique as the person bearing it. I, for example, compensated by putting on a show of confidence, competence, and efficiency. I came across as a controlling perfectionist. Looking back, I can see I was quite intimidating.

What no one else saw was that on the inside I felt unworthy, insignificant, incapable, and afraid—afraid that someone would find out my secret and declare me a fake, a hypocrite. It was a constant battle every day. Some days I played the part well, other days I couldn't keep up the facade. On those days, the emotions inside bubbled to the surface and exploded on anyone in my path. These outbursts only confirmed how I truly felt about myself. Admitting any faults felt like failure, so I had to appear good and right all the time, no matter whom I might hurt. I have made my husband, children, and friends suffer with me for my past sexual sin. They have been my unsuspecting victims.

Half a Cure Is Not Enough

Whether we enter into it voluntarily or have it forced upon us, sexual sin causes severe wounds and scars that need more than forgiveness. They require *healing* as well. That's why, even though I asked God to forgive me many times, my heart still felt ripped apart and closed off. Thankfully, God ended my insanity by showing me that healing was as important as forgiveness. My healing involved breaking the sexual bonds I had created that were impacting my life, even twenty-five years later. Throughout Scripture, God expresses His desire to heal us, as well as to forgive us. "If my people, who are called by my name, will humble themselves and pray and seek my face and turn from their wicked ways, then will I hear from heaven and will forgive their sin and will heal their land" (2 Chronicles 7:14).

God is eager to heal anything in your life that has been broken by sin: your heart, your soul, your reputation, your marriage, your family, your _____ (you fill in the blank). What's the "land" that you want God to heal in your life?

Examples in which forgiveness and healing are paired together are also evident in the New Testament. Jesus performed many miracles of physical healing for the people, but in almost every case He blessed them with something they weren't expecting—forgiveness. For example, the man lowered through the roof got more than he anticipated (Matthew 9:2–8). I believe the same is implied in the healings of the bleeding woman (Matthew 9:20–22) and the blind man (Mark 10:46–52). By putting healing and forgiveness together, Jesus was showing that in addition to physical healing, the recipients were also receiving the eternal *healing*—invisible healing—of their souls, which came through forgiveness.

In chapter 6, I'll help you begin your journey to healing and forgiveness by explaining the process of breaking sexual bonds. I say "begin" because I'm going to give you a starting point in this healing process. Where you go from there is up to you and God. Your journey of healing will look different from mine, because your past is different from mine. I can say with certainty, though, that our beginnings and endings will look the same. We all begin by surrendering to whatever God wants to do in us, and the journey will end with healed and forgiven hearts and lives.

I Hear You

As I ripped those paper hearts apart that night I saw it on their faces. They knew the pain of sexual sin. They felt the shame, the regret, the emptiness. They had hearts that needed healing, sins that needed forgiving, and sexual bonds that needed breaking.

"How can I break those bonds?" each of them inquired, some aloud, some silently, all with pain-filled eyes.

I can hear you asking that same question.

Have you created sexual bonds outside of marriage? Is your heart torn apart by your personal experiences of sexual bonding? I have good news of hope for you. You can be free from the sexual baggage that those bonds have created.

Let's begin by examining how sexual bonding happens and how it impacts us physically, emotionally, and spiritually.

UNDERSTANDING THE SEXUALLY BONDED HEART

How Does It Happen?

S exual bonding.

Whenever I say those words in any circle—on any continent!—heads turn and ears perk up. Regardless of the number or gender of the people present, just two words can render a room quiet. Before I know it, people are circled around me eager to discover what the words mean.

Why is this concept so intriguing? I believe it's because so few people my generation or younger have refrained from sexual compromise. Men and women, believers and unbelievers—all types of people have been affected by our culture's trends over the last few decades. Our beliefs, thoughts, and behavior about sex have for so long been influenced by the sexual revolution that most of us don't even recognize that anything is wrong.

That is, until you mention sexual bonding. That gets everyone's attention. Especially at the emotional level. Even among those who *think* or *believe* that sex outside of marriage is okay, I have yet to speak to even one who engaged in premarital sex who doesn't have feelings of regret, pain, and sadness over some aspect of the relationship or the breakup.

Most likely, I've evoked some feelings in you as well. They could be feelings of intrigue, hope, skepticism, or pain.

People long to find explanations for their pain. They ask questions. The three questions I hear most frequently are:

- What is sexual bonding?
- How does it happen?
- How can I break sexual bonds?

I hope I answered the first question in chapter 2. Now in this chapter my goal is to answer the second question: How does sexual bonding happen?

The Brain and Sex

Did you know that the brain is your most important sex organ? Physiologically, everything that happens to us sexually begins in the brain. That's where arousal and desire originate, and it's where the physical ability to act on that arousal is commanded.

Dr. Douglas Weiss,[1] a noted expert on sexual addiction and pornography, has researched the brain and sex and provides us with incredible insight about how we become bonded sexually. As with all organs in our body, the brain has chemical needs. Two of the chemicals that the brain produces and releases are endorphins and enkephalins. These chemicals act as natural pain relievers. They also give one an incredible sense of well-being.

There are several "pathways" by which these chemicals are released into the brain. One is through the runner's or aerobic high. Maybe you have experienced that sense of well-being after working out. Or maybe you have "hit the wall" in a marathon. This happens for some around mile twenty in a twenty-six-mile marathon. I've been told that it's that moment when a runner experiences the most extreme exhaustion and pain, the point at which one just can't take any more. If the runner pushes through this wall, the result is a burst of energy, as though the race has just begun. The reason is the release of endorphins and enkephalins into the bloodstream.

The other pathways are not as well known, but I'm sure you have experienced some of them. They include creative expression, artistic expression, close and intimate conversation, and sexual release. For many, the temptation to use repeatedly only one pathway to release these chemicals can cause unbalanced living. I think this is one of the reasons we see people addicted to various activities, such as working, shopping, and sex.

A healthy and balanced lifestyle includes a variety of pathways for releasing these chemicals. All of the pathways are appropriate for any age and any lifestyle. Except the pathway of sexual release. This one is unique. The sexual pathway involves a conditioning component that includes arousal. This isn't true of any of the other pathways.

Conditioning is a biological reality demonstrated by a famous scientist named Ivan Petrovich Pavlov. If you've taken any psychology courses, you've heard of him and his slobbering dogs. Through his research Pavlov discovered that our brains have the amazing ability to be conditioned or trained. We can train our brains to anticipate certain events associated with a "trigger." The trigger is any kind of signal or condition that can be detected through any of our senses.

Pavlov broke new scientific ground when he experimented with a dog, a bell, and some food and discovered for the world the conditioning capacity of the brain. Whenever the dog ate, he would salivate. Salivation is an involuntary response to food. We don't have to think about salivating. Our body does it naturally to help digestion.

But Pavlov was able to condition the dog's brain to cause salivation in response to a non-food stimulus. In a controlled environment, Pavlov would repeatedly ring the bell just before feeding the dog. What Pavlov discovered was that within a short period of time, the dog would begin to salivate as soon as he heard the bell ring, without even seeing the food.

Pavlov called this a "conditioned" or "trained response." The bell signaled the dog that food was on its way. The brains of dogs and people can be conditioned to respond to any number of triggers in anticipation of a variety of types of pleasure or pain.

By similar methods, Dr. Weiss explains, we can train our brains to respond to certain triggers in anticipation of sexual pleasure. Arousal, like salivation, is an involuntary response, and it happens when we believe that sexual pleasure is near. But arousal can be triggered by a wide variety of external triggers. Whatever you are looking at—or imaging in your mind—when you experience sexual release becomes your trigger for arousal. Over time, that object, person, or image that you've looked at or thought about during sexual release becomes your signal that sexual pleasure is coming, And each time you see or imagine your trigger, it can fire off the arousal response.

Your brain bonds with your trigger.

Sexual Bonding God's Way

Now here's the good news. When you save your brain as well as your body for your marriage partner, the person who is best able to trigger the arousal response is that person, and no other person or image causes quite the same response. I love to see very old couples who take obvious delight in each other. You've seen them; they still hold hands, kiss enthusiastically, and laugh at each other's jokes.

People like Joe and Anne, a couple in their sixties. I met them at a home show booth in my town. Joe was selling me on his expert house painting abilities. Anne looked on, smiling and nodding in agreement. The next week Joe came to my home to give me an estimate. As he was leaving, he told me to call his wife if I wanted to schedule him for the work. Then he said these amazing words, words we'd all love to hear: "I've been married to that woman for forty-seven years, and she still makes my knees weak."

I can hear you *ahhhing* right now. Every time I tell that story to a group of teenagers, all the girls swoon at such tender words from someone still so passionate about his wife. Joe and Anne are an excellent example of sexual bonding God's way. Even after the hair has turned gray, the waistline has expanded, and body parts have sunk or shrunk, they are still the most beautiful human beings on the earth to each other.

But if you're like me, your bonding experience hasn't been like that of Joe and Anne. Whether the story includes sexual abuse, rape, homosexuality, pornography, sexual promiscuity, or sex with your spouse before you got married—all of these create sexual bonds that impact your life and your relationships today. Even your relationship with God.

So what about us, the ones who—whether by choice or by force—didn't do it God's way? What if we're not like Joe and Anne? How have our brains been conditioned by bonding to other people or images?

Bonding to Pornography

Debbie was marrying the man of her dreams. But neither of them was aware that he was bringing something into their marriage that would have enormous sexual, emotional, and spiritual consequences. You see, Tom was involved with pornography before he got married, experiencing sexual release using images. Without even knowing it, he had become bonded to those images over time. As with most men I talk to, he thought it was no big deal; it wasn't going to affect his sexual relationship with his wife. In fact, he declared, he wouldn't need the pornography once he was married. Right? Not with a beautiful woman by his side to have sex with. Hopefully every night!

Wrong. To both of their surprise and dismay, Debbie couldn't turn Tom on. Why not? Because his brain had been conditioned to respond to a different arousal trigger—an image on the Internet, not his beautiful wife. Even though he could perform sexually, there was no feeling of sexual excitement attached to it for him. Unable to understand why, Tom would find himself leaving his wife in the middle of the night and finding sexual release—this holy, God-sanctioned gift to married soul-mates—with an inanimate object. Alone. In the dark. In secrecy and shame.

Another woman, named Becky, approached me at a women's retreat, after a seminar on sexual bonding. Armed with new information from the seminar, she was beginning to understand why her sexual relationship in her second marriage was in serious trouble. She was in the habit of using pornographic images to help her reach arousal—much to her husband's discomfort. She didn't understand why she needed them…until she learned about the brain and bonding. In her previous marriage, Becky's first husband had liked to use adult films to heighten the excitement during their lovemaking. Because of the conditioning she had undergone, Becky's brain now needed the pornography in order to become aroused. Even though Becky was madly in love with Husband Number Two, he couldn't arouse her sexually, and she needed the pornography to help her get in the mood.

How sad and tragic, to be married to the love of your life—your soul mate—and not be aroused by him or her. This kind of conditioning destroys marriages, devastates families, and hurts the very ones we love the most. This wasn't God's plan for us.

Pornography is in my opinion the greatest evil the human race has ever known. What begins as occasional, innocent pleasure rapidly progresses to addictive obsession, and eventually to perversion and violence. In the United States alone, pornography is a ten-billion-dollar business, and the profit margin is climbing. Even large, familiar, household-name companies—with whom you and I probably do business—share in this lucrative "industry." The greatest evil is that pornographers aim their business at very young people—even children under ten. They know that a young person addicted to their product will become a customer for life.

Dr. Judith Reisman,[2] an expert on pornography, child abuse, and brain imaging—and a personal friend of mine—states in an article on pornographic imaging that "sophisticated, medical diagnostic techniques confirm that images override text for brain dominance, and research indicates that a pornographic environment colonizes in a viewer's brain, producing structural changes in the brain that are involuntary and can last for years." That very sophisticated language is saying, more simply, that pornography actually alters brain chemistry. Dr. Reisman goes on to explain that the younger a viewer of pornographic images, the greater and more permanent the damage to the brain.

God has a word of warning for those who would stoop to hurt ones He calls "the least of these" (Matthew 25:40, 45)—the children, the disadvantaged, the powerless. He says, "It would be better for him to be thrown into the sea with a millstone tied around his neck than for him to cause one of these little ones to sin" (Luke 17:2). I believe Judgment Day is coming for those who make, film, distribute, and sell pornography.

To those whose sexual innocence has been snatched away by pornography, God speaks words of healing. He says (my paraphrase), "Come to Me and I will forgive all your sins, heal all your diseases, release you from your pit of hell, and crown you with love and compassion instead of shame and disgrace" (see Psalm 103:3–4).

Breaking sexual bonds might only be the first step in your journey to complete healing. You may also need counseling by experts in the area of sexual addiction and pornography. God knows exactly what you need, and as you surrender it to Him, He will guide you to the right places and the right people.

God offers forgiveness, grace, mercy, love, and healing to those victimized by pornography. But we can only receive these gifts if we lay the pornography and our addiction at His feet with a surrendered and repentant heart.

Bonding to Real People

Maybe you're not bonded to fake people, but to real people. People you know. People you loved and trusted. Someone you were sure you'd spend your life with. But didn't.

Or maybe people you encountered only once. A prostitute. A one-night stand. A back bedroom at a drinking party. A rapist.

How does bonding happen with people?

Remember the paper hearts? When I tore apart the two bonded hearts, neither one came away whole. Each took with it part of the other heart, firmly attached. That's what happens when we become bonded to real people. We may leave them physically, but emotionally, spiritually, and mentally we take them with us into our next relationship.

The bonding experience itself, while the relationship exists, can be a painful experience or a pleasant one. If it's painful, then the adverse emotions that accompanied that relationship—anger, hurt, betrayal, abandonment, shame, humiliation, or feeling used—will wound and scar our hearts. The wounds cause us to be more cautious, inhibiting our ability to be as open and trusting in the next relationship. Without realizing it, in order to protect ourselves from being hurt again, we give less and less of ourselves emotionally. In the new relationship, many of the other person's actions and words will unexpectedly touch the old, unhealed wounds. In an instant, our minds flash back to a previous lover, we experience the pain all over again, and we retreat into survival mode. We are prone to lash out at the new "offender" in our attempts at self-preservation.

My father, who passed away several years ago, broke his wrist as a young man playing hockey. Years later, even though that bone had healed, a visible line on his X-ray still showed where the break had been. The injury had left a scar. Most of the time, his wrist was pain free. But every once in a while, when he used it a certain way, he experienced discomfort or pain.

That's just what our sexually bonded hearts feel. The negative emotions may seem to heal with time, but in reality they've left invisible scars, which cry out in pain when "jostled" by flashbacks from past relationships. The pain causes us to do everything we can to protect those scars from further injury. So we close up or withdraw to protect ourselves.

I've experienced this myself. Unaware of what I was doing, I erected invisible walls to guard from further pain. I shut down my feelings completely. I would no longer allow myself to be so vulnerable as to let someone hurt me. Eventually I lost the ability to feel anything—pain, sadness, or even joy. Inside, I contained it all within one giant ball of indifference, fooling myself, believing that I was safe from harm.

How sad. I lost the rich emotional experience of all those years—the experience of being alive. I could sit through the saddest movie or hear the most tragic news—it made no difference. Tears seldom ran down this face. This heart of stone was not easily moved.

Until God healed me. Now the tears flow freely. I gladly experience extreme sadness and ecstatic joy. I cry when I worship God, I cry when I hear sad stories or watch sad movies. I cry for others when they're hurting. And I *love* it. I'm not afraid to feel anymore. I feel alive for the first time in many years. God gave me this promise from Ezekiel 36:26–27: "I will give you a new heart and put a new spirit in you; I will remove from you your heart of stone and give you a heart of flesh. And I will put my Spirit in you and move you to follow my decrees and be careful to keep my laws." And move me He does—to love again, to feel again, to cry again, and to laugh with real joy again.

Do you have an unmovable heart of stone? Or do you only allow your emotional and physical vulnerability with your spouse to progress a short distance before the wall goes up?

Would you like to feel again with a heart of flesh? Yes? Then hang in there. God has booked you for open-heart surgery!

It Felt So Right

Maybe the residue of a painful past relationship is easy to understand. But what if your past relationship was a pleasant experience? Then your sexual bonding may be associated with positive memories or feelings. How can this kind of bonding have damaging effects on future relationships?

Let's see how this plays out in the experience of a woman named Helen. Disillusioned with her present husband, she finds herself fantasizing about a past lover. However, the sexual bonding process has distorted the fantasy so that it no longer resembles the reality of that relationship. All Helen remembers is the wonderful, loving feelings she had for this man. She has begun to obsess about being with him again, imagining how her life would be different if she had married him, rather than her husband. The sexual bond to this past lover is beginning to erode her love for her present husband. If Helen doesn't break the bonds to her previous lover, they could eventually lead to the breakup of her marriage.

I recently appeared as a guest on a talk radio program. I was supposed to be talking about teenage sexual abstinence, but—as often happens—the host quickly gravitated to the subject of sexual bonding. I gave only a brief explanation of the cause and effect of sexual bonding, but it was all one listener needed to help her understand what was happening in her life. Her name was Sandra, and she spoke on behalf of many listeners that day when she said to me, "You just described my whole life. I began having sex when I was fourteen, and now I'm a twenty-four-year-old single mom." She went on to say that even though her past relationships were not all positive, when she is feeling lonely and sad, her bonding to past lovers causes her to fantasize about being with them again. She said, "I definitely feel emotionally and spiritually bonded to my past lovers. I can identify with everything you've said."

After a sexual bonding seminar, another woman named Lynne wanted to speak to me. "My problem is that as a teenager I was very pretty and popular with the boys." That was easy to believe, considering how she looked at forty. "I found this to be an advantage for me," she explained. "Flirting with the boys was a powerful rush."

Lynne's flirting led to a sexually promiscuous lifestyle that lasted for many years. But as an adult, even though she felt forgiven for her past, she still had a strong urge to flirt with other men, despite her happy fifteen-year marriage. Enlightened by the seminar, Lynne began to see how she was bonded to the feelings of power, acceptance, and desirability that her past flirting and sexual conquests had created in her. Her past bonding experiences were positive, but were keeping her tied to past destructive behavior. With tears welling up and a heart full of pain, Lynne expressed that she wanted to be released from this need to feel desirable to other men. She wanted her husband's desire to be enough.

Stolen Innocence

As you can see, sexual bonding is a multifaceted phenomenon. The ways it happens and the ways it affects us are more numerous then we can explain here. For many reading this book, sexual bonding began as a child. Maybe this happened to you against your will. If that's true, I'm so sorry.

We'd like to believe that, because the child is an involuntary victim, he or she would not be subject to sexual bonding. Unfortunately, a child can begin to feel close and intimate with the offender, even though it is an unpleasant— often horrifying—experience. If you were sexually abused as a child, your sexual pathway was opened early in life. The result may be that the need to feel close and intimate in your teenage or adult relationships has propelled you to initiate sex. After all, that's what you experienced as love early on. Many victims of sexual abuse continue into very promiscuous lifestyles, often leading to pregnancy and abortion.

For you, breaking sexual bonds will only be a part of your complete healing. In addition, you will very likely need counseling or victim support groups to allow God's complete healing to permeate your soul. Part of your healing will be allowing God to show you how subsequent choices in your life were driven by your abuse.

But there's hope for everyone. Regardless of the cause and effect of sexual bonding in your life, God can heal it *all*.

Oxytocin—Human Superglue

We've talked about endorphins and enkephalins, which are released in our brains during sex. Our bodies produce yet another chemical—a hormone called oxytocin—that is related to our sexual relationships. This is another example illustrating God's design for lifelong bonding to one person among humans.

Oxytocin is produced by the pituitary gland, and we experience high levels of it in three types of circumstances: during labor and delivery, while breastfeeding, and during sexual arousal and release. In their article "Bonding Imperative"[3] Dr. Eric J. Keroack and Dr. John R. Diggs, Jr., of the Medical Abstinence Council, explain that animal research has revealed that nesting behavior in birds, cub-rearing behavior in bears and lions, and lifetime mating in prairie voles are all related to high brain levels of oxytocin. New data is also supporting the theory that this hormone plays a key role in human attachments. Scientific studies show that levels of oxytocin rose threefold in men during erection and orgasm, but if oxytocin-blocking agents were used, the sexual sensations and feelings were blocked as well. The men were able to "complete the task," but without any sexual desire attached to the event. Doctors Keroack and Diggs suggest that "this is why men who damage their bonding mechanism through casual sex are less able to form lifetime commitments to their mates."

"In women," Diggs and Keroack explain, "a small preliminary study showed that being in a stable, positive relationship was associated with more responsive elevations of oxytocin blood levels to pleasant relationship memories. Oxytocin levels were unchanged during recall of negative emotional experiences. On the other hand, women with relationships characterized by anxiety had flat responses to positive memories and lower oxytocin levels with negative memories. This suggests that previous relationship experiences can alter 'sexual bonding' by altering the release of the biochemical 'superglue.' If the relationship history is sufficiently adverse, this study shows that women will lose their ability to bond."

But the most interesting finding, say Keroack and Diggs, is that oxytocin inhibits the development of tolerance in opiate receptors in the brain. Remember the endorphins and enkephalins? Well, that "wow" feeling from sex is partially created by these chemicals. But as the relationship matures, fewer endorphins are released, so their effect decreases.

It's the same kind of thing that happens when we take addictive drugs. As time goes on we need higher doses of the drug to create that euphoric sensation. "But what is fascinating about oxytocin," says Diggs and Keroack, "is that if a sexual relationship is well bonded, the oxytocin response helps maintain the 'wow' even though fewer endorphins are released." Oxytocin can help keep the love alive, long into the relationship."

"Unfortunately," continue the authors, "people who have misused their sexual faculty and become bonded to multiple persons will diminish the power of oxytocin to maintain a permanent bond with an individual. Because, just as in heroin addiction, when the receptors become accustomed to a certain level of endorphins, in the absence of oxytocin, the person involved will experience 'sex withdrawal,' and will need to move on to a 'new and more exciting' environment, that is, a new sex playmate."

We have all heard of sexual addicts. The endorphins and enkephalins that are released during sex are addicting. They are so pleasurable that we want to repeat the activity over and over again. God designed the presence of oxytocin to ensure that we want to repeat it with the same person—our spouse—thereby protecting us from becoming sexually addicted. Sounds like a perfect plan, doesn't it?

Let me share this illustration from Keroack and Diggs. Imagine taking a big piece of duct tape. Stick it to the hairiest part of your arm. Now pull it off. *Ouch.* Look at all that hair attached to the tape. Now put it on another hairy part of your body. This time when you pull it off, there's not quite as much stickiness as before, and less hair comes away with the tape. As you continue to do this, you will find that the tape will lose its adhesive ability altogether. That's what it's like with the hormone oxytocin. With the first sexual partner, there is significant bonding, but with each subsequent sexual partner—including marriage partners—the hormone's binding power diminishes.

Just last week, I was reading an article in a popular magazine that described a fascinating new phenomenon. Today, a surprising number of people are seeking out their high school sweethearts, years after graduation, and often after having married and divorced someone else. These individuals feel an especially close connection with their first lovers—a connection that they weren't able to duplicate in subsequent relationships.[4] Could the reason be that, regardless of the way the high school relationship ended, that was the one relationship in these people's experience that was most highly "oxytocin-drenched," and so the bond with the original lover remains strong enough to influence heart and mind for many years?

Is it a surprise then, in a culture compromised by sexual promiscuity and multiple partners, to find the divorce rate so high? By our bonding with other people and objects in the past, we've reduced our ability to physically and emotionally bond with the one we finally choose as a life partner. My heart breaks when I hear men and women say, after multiple broken relationships and marriages, "There's something wrong with me. I can't seem to have a normal relationship. I guess I'm just not the marrying kind."

I'm sorry, but that's nonsense—a lie of the enemy. In most cases it's not *who we are*, but *what we've done*, that is messing up our relationships. In the next chapter, we'll talk more about how premarital sex impacts our ability to form close and intimate relationships with God and others. For now, let me assure you that divorce is not a virus you catch or a congenital disease you can inherit. Even if you've had several divorces, or if your family is littered with them, you can begin right now to take steps to significantly increase your chances that the next marriage (if you're single) or the present one (if you're married) is the one in which you keep your vows.

Until death do you part.

THE HEART'S CRY FOR INTIMACY

The Impact of Sexual Bonding on Relationships

Dear Abby: I desperately need some guidance because I'm afraid I'm putting myself in grave danger. I lost my virginity when I was sixteen to a boy I hardly knew. I am now twenty and off to college, and I have literally lost count of the number of men I have had sex with. Only a handful of them have actually been boyfriends.

I always feel horrible and used after sex, not to mention that I am constantly worried about STDs and pregnancy since I never use protection. Yet I can't stop being promiscuous, and I can't settle down with any one person. My self-worth has disintegrated, and sex has become meaningless to me.

Abby, please set me straight. I'm so lost and don't know who to confide in. Scared and Ashamed in Washington, *Sacramento Bee*, July 19, 2004

I'm so lost.

I feel horrible and used.

I can't stop being promiscuous.

My self-worth has disintegrated.

Sex has become meaningless to me.

I'm afraid.

I'm desperate.

I'm so lost.

Can you hear her sense of forlorn abandonment? Can you feel her broken, empty, heart-wrenching pain?

Sexual promiscuity is one of the relational consequences of inappropriate sexual bonding. In chapter 2, I quoted from the research of Dr. Donald Joy, where he explained that sex leads to more sex.[1] In other words, we long for bonding experiences from the past, so we try to recreate them in subsequent relationships, and we initiate sex sooner and sooner. Studies show that the earlier a teenager begins to have sex, the more sexual partners each one will have in a lifetime.[2] These relationships are generally shorter, and those who engage in them have time and opportunity for several before they eventually marry.

The consequences of sexual promiscuity are enormous. Working at a Pregnancy Resource Center, I see it all. Sexually transmitted diseases (STDs), non-marital pregnancy, and abortion are some of the outward, visible consequences. What I hear from those wounded by sexual promiscuity is that the greater damage is what happens inside. Our "Scared and Ashamed" friend in Washington articulates emotions many of us may long deny.

She speaks for you.

She speaks for me.

She speaks the truth.

True Intimacy and Its Counterfeit

There are many reasons why people get divorced. I suggest that sexual bonding before marriage is one of the contributing factors. Consider this: In 1960 the divorce rate was approximately 25 percent; today it's 50 percent.[3] In forty years the divorce rate has doubled. What's interesting is that the rate of sexual promiscuity has increased in proportion to the divorce rate.

I didn't need to convince Alan about this parallel; he's lived it. He's been married twice and divorced twice. Sexual promiscuity was just part of his everyday life. After all, that's what everyone did in relationships, right? By the time I met Alan, he had become a Christian and was looking for a new way to build a relationship that honored God and would hopefully last forever. It was no coincidence we met; I'm confident it was a carefully orchestrated plan of God. What I was teaching in my abstinence program was exactly what this thirty-year-old, twice-divorced man with two children needed to hear.

Alan was desperate not to repeat his past mistakes. He and his two children had suffered enough. And yet Alan still didn't know what he was doing wrong or how he could do it differently next time. God had some words of hope for him. As I shared with him about sexual bonding and its impact on relationships, he began the process of breaking those bonds so that his next relationship could be free from the negative impact of his past. But Alan also had to come to understand that he was using sex in his relationships to take the place of true intimacy. He had to learn the role of genuine intimacy in the building of a lasting relationship.

In chapter 2, I mentioned briefly the concept of *true intimacy*—the desire we have for someone to know and love us for who we are. This is a desire put inside us by God Himself, and it can only be ultimately and completely filled by Him. But here on earth, God has graciously blessed us with the experience of true intimacy with others as well. We call them soul mates or best friends. True intimacy is one of the qualities of a great marriage, and we ideally hope to achieve it with our spouses. Unfortunately, nonmarital sex has become a cheap imitation of true intimacy in our culture. It can make us feel close even when we hardly know each other.

In his book *The Intimacy Cover-Up,*[4] marriage and family therapist Roger Hillerstrom describes how intimacy spans a range of five increasing levels of vulnerability:

Level One: Lowest Level

The lowest level is where we share what Hillerstrom calls superficial reports or factual statements like:

"It's a nice day."

"The Kings won last night."

"That view is gorgeous."

When a relationship consists primarily of superficial interaction like this, it's not very deep.

Level Two: Low Level

Hillerstrom says this is the level where we offer third-party perspectives and beliefs:

"Yesterday I was reading in the paper…"

"My grandma always used to say…"

"My friend believes…"

Hillerstrom says that at this level we are sharing a piece of ourselves by quoting from those with whom we associate. We are not directly divulging anything about ourselves, however, and are therefore safe from others criticizing or rejecting us. This level is only slightly more vulnerable than level one.

Level Three: Moderate Level

This is where we begin to open up about ourselves, where we begin to share our own perceptions and beliefs:

"I believe abortion is wrong."

"I think Christians should be proactive in politics."

"I believe in traditional marriage."

At this level we tell others what we think about things. And if the person we're telling is important to us or if we want to avoid conflict or rejection, we may be willing to change our opinion if we sense disapproval. Or at least we'll *say* that we've changed it.

Level Four: High Level

Now we get personal and intimate. Hillerstrom says that at this level we begin to share our personal history—things we've done and choices we've made, good or bad.

"My greatest accomplishment was to win a national journalism award."

"I've had more sexual partners than I can count."

"When I was 21, I had an abortion."

We're taking a chance here. If we're rejected at this level, we can't change our minds or retract what we've said, because we can't change our history. If we sense disapproval, all we can do is try to make others believe that we've changed.

Level Five: Highest Level

This is where genuine intimacy lies, Hillerstrom says. It's where we share our feelings and emotional reactions—those that are most precious and most fragile.

"I'm hurt by what you said."

"I'm angry about what you did."

"The way you treat me, I feel so special."

The risk at this level is that if others reject our feelings, needs, and emotional reactions, we have no escape as in levels one through four; we must simply absorb or respond to the pain.

Our deepest feelings and emotions don't change quickly. What I'm feeling at my core today will be there tomorrow as well. So there's a risk that if you reject me today, you'll also reject me tomorrow. The other scary part is that people can use our vulnerable feelings against us later. Repeated injuries are often even more painful than the first time.

To get to this level we need to develop deep trust in the other person. We trust that they will accept our emotions, needs, and feelings, and still love us just as we are.

How (and How Not) to Achieve Intimacy

True intimacy occurs when both people meet each other at the same level, then progress together to deeper levels of vulnerability. This takes time. Often, partners can be at different levels. For example, one may be communicating at the high level, sharing personal history, and the other may be sharing at the moderate level, divulging only opinions. This can give a false sense of intimacy.

The healthiest and truest intimacy develops when the

partners grow together. Relationships in which partners communicate in both directions at the highest level of intimacy are those in which the partners have slowly, progressively built a solid foundation of friendship. It's like losing weight. Slower weight loss requires a lifestyle change and is more likely to be permanent. It involves building a foundation of habits that will continue to produce results. Relationships that have the greatest chance of lasting are the ones that have built a foundation of intimate communication.

Unfortunately, in our culture we've exchanged intimacy through communication with counterfeit "intimacy" through sex. The results have been disastrous.

Whenever I speak, I always ask people, "At what level of intimacy do you think people should be when they start having sex?" The answer is always the same—the highest level.

But then I ask, "At what level do you think most people are when they start having sex in a relationship?"

How would you answer? If you would say what most people say—the low to moderate level—you're right. Isn't it amazing? People having sex when they hardly know each other? According to Hillerstrom, when people start having sex while communicating only at the moderate level of vulnerability, they are unable to progress to the highest level until they backtrack and do the communication work they've skipped over.[5]

What? I can hear your reaction. If you're finding this hard to believe, it's because once you started having sex, your relationship began to *feel* close, when it actually wasn't very close at all. In this situation, your relationship begins to focus on the physical. Rather than growing in intimacy through communication, you begin to "communicate" through sex.

Hillerstrom uses an illustration[6] to describe what happens. He says that a relationship is like a steam pipe that has tiny hairline cracks that you can't see with the natural eye. Whenever two people come together, they bring differences into the relationship—differences in values, beliefs, backgrounds, opinions...the list is endless. No matter how much the partners love each other, these differences cause conflict. Conflict is the steam rushing through the relational pipe.

Now, at the end of the pipe is a valve—the sexual relationship. If the valve is open—meaning the couple is having sex—the steam flows through, the pressure is relieved, and the couple believes they've resolved the conflict. In reality, they've simply delayed dealing with the real problems. The couple *feels* as though everything is okay, because the sex has made them feel close.

But unfortunately, those tiny hairline cracks begin to corrode, while the couple continues unaware of the need for relational maintenance. Because their attention hasn't been drawn to the cracks, the cracks will eventually begin to erode the pipe—the relationship. When enough conflicts build up, the sex is no longer able to provide the temporary respite, and resentment escalates. Since the couple has never developed the habit of healthy communication to resolve conflicts, the relationship disintegrates. Sex distracts the partners from the need for relational maintenance, which can only be accomplished by means of true conflict resolution—focused, cooperative attention to the cracks.

But if you close that valve—stop having sex in the relationship—what happens? The steam is forced to escape through those tiny hairline cracks, and the partners' attention is drawn to them. This makes it more difficult for the couple to avoid dealing with the relationship's real needs. The problems, conflicts, and differences are unavoidably exposed, and the couple is more likely to do the hard work, starting to communicate and to resolve the problems in a way that produces results.

Sex only puts a Band-Aid on the wound. Communication is the salve that allows it to heal.

Hillerstrom counsels hundreds of couples who either are seeking to get married or are already married. He tells those who are having sex before marriage to stop so they can move to that highest level of intimacy in their relationship and ensure a lifelong marriage. Couples who follow his guidance discover the unexpected benefit of closing the sex valve. They learn for the first time to communicate love in nonphysical ways. To love with words through letters and cards. To love with meaningful gifts or acts of service. To love with gifts of time, communication, and praise. All these expressions of love become the bricks that gradually build a solid foundation for a marriage. But the couple misses this critical relational dimension completely if they continue using sex alone to communicate love.

This message was not lost on Alan. Several months after we talked, he introduced me to a young woman he was starting to date. He shared with her what he had learned about building a relationship God's way, and she was equally eager not to repeat her past mistakes. I had the opportunity to meet with them and give them the tools, not only to give this relationship the best chance of survival, but also to break their bonds with their past sexual relationships. As I write this, Alan and Krista are preparing to get married. They've built their relationship to the highest level of intimacy by saving sex for their wedding night. After several painful divorces between the two of them, they finally realized that their failures were not because of who they were, but because of what they had failed to build into their past marriages—true emotional intimacy.

A New Kind of Fast

Now, are you ready for this? Sexual abstinence is not only valuable for unmarried couples; it can also be a good idea for us married folk.

What? Celibacy in marriage?

Well, yes. But only for a limited time and for a specific purpose. In his counseling practice, Hillerstrom[7] instructs couples who have had sex before marriage, and who are therefore struggling in their marriage relationships, to abstain from having sex for a time, in order to allow their relationship to grow to intimacy level five. Sounds a little bizarre doesn't it? How can a married couple, sleeping in the same bed at night, avoid sex night after night and talk instead? It sounded a little far-fetched to me as well. Great in theory, but impossible in practice.

God thought otherwise.

You see, my husband and I didn't save sex for marriage. When I learned about the importance of nonsexual communication, I realized we had not yet reached the highest level of intimacy in our relationship. But I ignored the nagging thought that we should abstain from sex in order to learn the communication lessons we missed before marriage. It was too crazy to even think about.

Until God spoke. Clear as a bell one day He said to me,

How can you advise others to do something you're not willing to do yourself? It was no longer a nagging thought, but a clear, compelling question. So I described to my husband what I felt God was urging us to try. I expected only incredulous opposition.

But he agreed!

I couldn't believe it. He thought it was silly, but he was willing to try. Since an open-ended sex fast seemed unwise, we set a reachable goal. We decided that on our twenty-third anniversary—one month away—we would come together again.

I didn't think one month would make much difference, but the experience was amazing for both of us. Through it, God taught me about another consequence of sexual bonding outside of marriage.

Those Debilitating Lies

What if I told you that many of the messages we've learned about sex are lies? Not glaring lies, but subtle ones. In fact, most of us have believed them for so long that to think any other way wouldn't feel right. Life is a teacher, and whether our lessons have come from watching others or from our own experiences, we have internalized them all. Some of our conclusions are true. But unfortunately, when it comes to sex, many of them are false.

We learn our life lessons as we sit in countless classrooms. We grow up in the context of our parents' dysfunctional marriage, their failure to teach us about sex, their promiscuity, and then the freedom they give us along with a condom, so that we can follow in their footsteps. We live through the experience of a lover (or many lovers) who use us for their pleasure.

There's our introduction to pornography. School teachers who impart their values about sex. Maybe someone older or more powerful forcing themselves upon us through rape or sexual abuse. And more.

In all these classrooms, and many others, the spoken and silent messages have engraved on our hearts lasting attitudes and values regarding sex that are deceptive, destructive lies. In 2 Corinthians 7:1, Paul says, "Let us purify ourselves from everything that contaminates body and spirit." Experiencing sex in any way other than according to God's plan contaminates body and spirit, leading us to live for years believing messages about sex that are blatantly false.

When, under the influence of these lies, we engage in nonmarital sex, we do ourselves invisible, internal injury, and this causes us to harden our hearts against God and others. The lies become a poison that invades every part of our souls—seeping into our friendships, our families, our marriages, and our beds.

After we've given ourselves away so often and so cheaply, we easily begin to feel used, dirty, worthless. We come to believe that because of our actions we are somehow less valuable. We also communicate that view subliminally to those around us, who confirm it by devaluing us further. We start out as a crisp, spotless designer piece in the display window at Nordstrom's, but end up feeling like a tattered discard on the clearance rack at the thrift store. Used up. Out of date. Unwanted.

It's a lie. Neither you nor any other human determines your value. God does. He assures us in Deuteronomy 7:6 that we are "his treasured possession," and there's nothing we can do to change His view of us.

One Sunday, our pastor took out a twenty-dollar bill and held it up for everyone to see. He asked if anyone wanted it. Hands shot up and cheers rang out.

Then he crumpled the bill, threw it on the floor, and ground it under his shoe. He held it up and again asked who wanted it now. The response was the same as before.

What was his point? He was demonstrating that no matter how dirty, crumpled, or torn the bill became, it still had the same value. The bill's worth was determined before it was even printed, and his mistreatment had not changed its value.

Your value has never changed. You are worth just as much today as on the day God created you. No matter how you've behaved or how you've been treated—like a brand-new designer piece or a thrift store bargain—you are and always have been a treasured possession of the One who created you. No one—not even you—can change that.

Exposing the Lies

God says that the first step in ridding ourselves of these lies is to bring them into the open. Mark 4:22 says, "For whatever is hidden is meant to be disclosed, and whatever is concealed is meant to be brought out into the open." Once they're in the open, God allows us to see them for what they really are. The main reason the enemy doesn't want you to tell anyone about your plight is that his power is in the secret. Secrecy prevents your exposure to the truth and keeps the lie alive. The enemy uses our secrets and lies against us, to rob us of all that God wants to give—joy, peace, contentment, love, forgiveness, healing, and wholeness. But God wants us to have open, intimate relationships with Him and others. When we open up, God is able to cleanse and purify our souls, bodies, and minds and to exchange the lies for His truth.

Lies destroy. God's truth gives life.

Are you ready for life? It's time to ask God to search your heart and shine His light on your innermost being.

"Impossible," I can hear some of you saying. "Darkness and secrecy are the only existence I know. It's what I'm comfortable with and what I've identified with as long as I can remember." Sadly, we would rather believe a lie than venture into unfamiliar territory—even into freedom and truth. Even into life.

I know. I've been there. But during our month-long sex fast, I worked through an exercise that helped me burst through the fear barrier. Let me share it with you.

I took the time to work through a series of enlightening questions from *The Path to Sexual Healing* by Linda Cochrane.[8] I've listed the questions below. They're designed to help a person see how sexual bonding has contaminated his or her soul with lies about sex, self, and others.

I know it may not be easy, but I encourage you to respond to each of these questions, as I did. And I want you to answer them as honestly as possible. The greater your vulnerability—to yourself and to God—the more valuable the healing insights you will gain.

Don't spend a lot of time thinking about any one answer. Just give your first yes-or-no response.

Ready? Go.

- Do you have difficulty expressing yourself sexually?
- Do you avoid times of intimacy?

- Do you struggle with lust?
- Do you sometimes feel powerless to assert or protect yourself against sexual harm?
- Do you feel unworthy of being loved or cared for in the way you need?
- Do you struggle with eating too much or too little?
- Do you feel ashamed of your body?
- Do you view your body as dirty, ugly, or bad?
- Do you have difficulty believing your body is a home for the Holy Spirit?
- Have you ever used drugs or alcohol as an emotional pain reliever?
- Have you ever needed drugs or alcohol to be able to express yourself sexually?
- Do you have any self-punishing behaviors?
- Have you ever chosen sexual partners outside of God's plan? (Remember, God's plan is no sexual partner until marriage, and then your spouse as your only sexual partner until death.)
- Have you ever been a victim of another person's sexual sin?
- Do you have a general mistrust of men or women?
- Are you tempted with sexual perversions?
- Are there any areas of your sexuality that are not in line with God's plan?
- Has your sexuality ever gone to the extremes of promiscuity or frigidity?
- Do you struggle with memories of past sexual sin?
- Are you aware of suffering from any consequences of your own sexual sin?

- Do you have habitual and progressively
  worsening destructive sexual habits?

Now look back over your answers. For each yes response, try to determine whether the behavior is a consequence of your sexual sin, and list it in the first space below. If it is a consequence of your victimization by another's sexual sin, list it under the second heading.

Consequences of my sexual sin:

Consequences of my victimization by someone else's sexual sin:

Now, here is one more set of questions. This time as you respond, I want you to take your time. Prayerfully consider your answers. You may not be able to address them all at once; they may open up painful memories that you didn't know you had stored away.

God wants to shine His light on the lies. Answering these questions honestly is the first step in allowing Him to do that.

- What did you learn from your mother about being a woman?
- What did you learn from your mother about sex?
- What did you learn from your father about being a man?
- What did you learn from your father about sex?
- What did you learn about sex from childhood friends, siblings, cousins, aunts, uncles, TV, or magazines?
- What sexual trauma did you experience as a child?
- As a teenager?
- As a young adult?
- As an adult?
- Which of these experiences caused you the most trauma?
- In which of these experiences were you the victim?
- Which of these experiences were caused by your own sin?
- What trauma from these experiences would you like God to heal?
- What do you remember about these experiences and what emotions do you associate with them?
- Was pornography involved in any of your relationships?
- How has watching pornography impacted your view of yourself and sex?

Okay, now go back over your answers again. What are some of the lies about sex, yourself, and others that have become ingrained in your thinking because of your experiences? How have those lies contributed to your attitude towards sex?

What I Learned About My Lies

As I answered those questions, God began to reveal some of the lies that I had embraced about sex, men, and myself through my experiences.

My very first sexual encounter was definitely traumatic. Even though it wasn't rape, it was done in haste and secrecy. This guy who was supposed to love me displayed little comfort or care for my feelings. I sensed his need to get the job done, regardless of my feelings. It was a humiliating experience that left me feeling extremely vulnerable. But I didn't realize that it had had this impact until years later, as I answered the questions from Linda Cochrane's book. Whatever feelings I experienced that day in my high school years must have been locked up tight, because this was the first I had become aware of them.

What did that long-past experience have to do with me right now?

Everything. God showed me that my view of sex had been shaped by it. Somewhere in the back of my conscience, sex was a humiliating and soul-baring experience, and guys didn't really care about your feelings as long as they got what they wanted. Unconsciously I had projected that attitude onto my husband and brought my negative impressions into our bed.

So the first thing I did was to ask God to break the bond that I had with that early experience and to heal the negative, damaging attitude I had towards sex and my husband. I needed to see sex in a whole new way—God's way. And indeed, throughout that month, He used my husband and His Word to transform my thoughts and feelings about sex.

I also had to confront the lies from a more recent source. The disgrace I felt for engaging in premarital sex with my husband had followed me into our marriage relationship. Instead of seeing sex with my husband as pure and positive, I associated our sexual experiences with negative emotions of guilt and shame. I agree that guilt and shame are appropriate responses to sexual sin, but God never intended that we miss out on the blessing of sex in marriage because of past negative associations.

Have you ever eaten something and then been sick? From that point on, you've associated that food with that horrible experience, haven't you? When I was eight years old, my family visited my aunt and uncle at Christmas. The traditional Scottish dumpling was served for breakfast, and right after I ate it I became very sick. Now whenever I smell or taste dumpling, I immediately revert to age eight, become sick to my stomach, and start throwing up. Since childhood, I have never been able to eat that particular dish.

This is a mental association. We can develop them around foods, music, experiences, emotions, and so on. If you've had a negative experience with sex, you will, from that point on, associate sex with all the emotions you felt in that instance. Humiliation, vulnerability, fear, distrust, guilt, shame, and feeling used are only a few of the emotions you may have experienced. The reemergence of these same emotions may be keeping you and your spouse from enjoying sex—that incredible blessing God wants you to enjoy in a loving, committed marriage.

We prevent this kind of association when we obey Him by saving sex for marriage. But as I learned during that month before our twenty-third anniversary, God also offers purifying healing when we expose the lies.

During my husband's and my month of sexual abstinence, wonderful things happened. I've just shared some of the life-changing fruit that God bore in my own heart and mind. But God also worked through the interaction between the two of us. We did talk more, and we began to share at a much deeper level then we had before. We grew in intimacy and got to know each other at a new level. Our love and romance was rekindled, and our commitment to one another was strengthened.

I sensed God's pleasure in our obedience, and in return He poured out amazing blessings on our relationship.

I'm now convinced these are blessings God desires for every married couple.

Recommended Racy Reading

One other important experience (during our sexual fast) helped reshape my attitudes about sex. And it simply involved reading the Bible.

Have you ever read the Song of Songs in the Old Testament? I never read it all the way through, and I never took it seriously, until Linda Cochrane, in her Bible study *The Path to Sexual Healing*,[9] encouraged me to read the entire book through every day, five days in a row. I didn't grasp the benefit until my second of the five readings. That's when God began to reveal to me that the only way to expose our internalized lies is to read the truth about sex. The Song of Songs is the expert book of all time on the topic. So I read it—five days of love and sex.

I had no idea God could be so sexy. He doesn't even blush as He describes the intimate sexual relationship between the "lover" (the husband) and the "beloved" (the wife). Does that make you a little uncomfortable—calling God "sexy"? Before I read the Song of Songs, I would have felt the same discomfort. But after studying it, there's no doubt in my mind that God made sex extremely sexy, fun, pleasurable, playful, fulfilling...and necessary. And He's not afraid to say so.

In the Song, the beloved and the lover can't seem to get enough of each other. They are always talking about sex, having sex, and describing their sexual delight. Their sexual relationship seems to be a priority, and they make a point of getting away together whenever they can so they can partake of its pleasure.

I was surprised to realize that the woman in the Song expressed desire for sexual intimacy as much as, or even more than, the man. That went against my sense of decency. Somewhere I had learned that women who like sex too much must be either abnormal or "too easy," or even—dare I say?—unwholesome. During my promiscuous days, I connected my desire and lack of restraint with immorality, something shameful. But right there in the Bible I saw that, according to God, desire and lack of restraint *within marriage* is a good thing. It's not something to be ashamed of, but something to celebrate!

Do you see how setting the truth up next to the lie exposes its fallacy?

God revealed one other important insight to me in this book. I noticed that the lover frequently praised and verbally admired his wife. The beloved surrendered her complete self to his love and responded willingly to his embrace. Since marriage is a living picture of our relationship with God (see Ephesians 5:31–33), Song of Songs reminds me that God is our Lover, and He pursues us with love and passion. We respond by surrendering everything to Him and falling into His embrace of love and grace.

But the lover's pursuit and the beloved's surrender also cast a new light on my relationship with my husband. God showed me that, rather than surrendering myself to my husband's love and embrace, I often withdrew. Why? My past had scarred me with a lack of trust in the arena of love and sex. To me, sex could not be an expression of love; sex could only be manipulative. True love was demonstrated in everything *but* sex—through gifts, time, and words of affirmation. Yes, those are all valid expressions of love. But when my husband wanted sex, I never connected it with him actually loving me—he just wanted sex. It was a physical need, not a way of expressing love or a desire for intimacy.

I was so wrong.

God showed me that this amazing gift of sex is, at the least, a pleasant physical act. At the most, it is emotional, spiritual, and psychological intimacy that offers comfort, nurture…love. It is the means to forging a unifying bond more powerful than anything else on earth for both the man and the woman.

My prior sexual bonding had hardened my heart toward God and others. I had built a wall to keep others out, to reduce the risk of further injury.

Seeing sex God's way softened my heart and defeated my fear of relationships—with God and with my husband. I was free to risk again.

Reading the truth further revolutionized our marriage. And I came to know God in a whole new way.

Now the Old Testament is at the top of my recommended reading list.

Your Unique Journey

The trauma of my past may be mild compared to yours. The lies imposed on you may be far more devastating and crippling—even horrendous. Regardless of what you have been through, I know for certain that God hears your cry of pain and has answers for you, just as He did for me.

The very best news I can offer is that God wants to restore everything the enemy has taken from you. Have courage, my friend, and trust.

Trust me, because I've been debilitated by the lies, afraid of intimate relationships. But now I am here. And believe me, the journey was worth it.

And trust God, because the One who longs for you and promises to heal you is faithful.

I guarantee it.

THE HEART'S CRY FOR HEALING

Why Forgiveness Is Only the Beginning

I just got off the phone. The person I was speaking with said something that sounded very familiar to me. It is the same thing I said a year ago: "But I have gone through the forgiveness. I don't want to deal with it anymore. Every time I think about it I feel bad. I just want to forget it now."

Maybe you are thinking that, too. Why dredge up the past and let it complicate your life now? It only hurts when you think about it. *So just don't think about it.*

Unfortunately, I found that advice impossible to follow. I couldn't keep the old, unhealed wounds from resurfacing. If I didn't resurrect them myself, someone or something else always reminded me. It was a tormenting, exhausting cycle.

First came the reminder. Then the feelings of regret and shame. Then pleading for God's forgiveness—again—hoping it would work this time, so I could forgive myself. Then feeling compelled to perform for God, in order to pay for my sins. And finally, finding no answers to my questions or relief from my pain, I'd stuff it all inside and act as though everything was great.

Until the *next* rude reminder.

Does this sound like your life?

After decades of this cycle of self-crucifixion, I came to the realization that I was missing a critical ingredient. It wasn't forgiveness that was missing. God says His forgiveness is free and immediate. First John 1:9 says, "If we confess our sins, he is faithful and just and will forgive us our sins and purify us from all unrighteousness." I had been completely forgiven from the first moment that I confessed my sin.

So why didn't I *feel* forgiven?

Because God wanted to perform a work in my heart that went beyond forgiveness. He wanted to *heal* me. For all those years, I didn't realize that there is a difference between forgiveness and healing.

I've already discussed the ways that sexual sin wounds and scars us. When we come to God in repentance, He forgives us instantly. But the emotional wounds remain, open and sensitive. Before we receive God's healing, the enemy pours shame, like salt, into those wounds to keep us constantly in pain. We try to numb the agony by means of countless self-destructive mechanisms that, for a short time, protect us and help us cope. But in the end these only increase our self-loathing, driving us deeper into the grips of self-destructive vices. Without healing, we can't forgive ourselves. And our self-condemnation keeps us from feeling the cleansing, restoring forgiveness of God.

I can hear you asking, "How does healing happen?"

Good question. Let me take you back to Scripture again for the answer. James 5:16 says, "Therefore confess your sins to each other and pray for each other so that you may be healed."

Healing begins when we tell our secrets to another person.

Inching into the Light

From the moment I began to surrender my past to God, He had wanted me to tell someone. Someone specific—my mother, of all people. I love my mother dearly, but telling her the worst about me was the last thing I wanted to do.

What is more, I somehow knew the telling wouldn't end with her. God was letting me know that I would also tell my children one day. I could begin to conceive of baring it all to my mother. But not my kids! The very thought of shattering forever my children's image of me made me want to die first.

The voice of God was strong. But I was afraid. The only person who knew the truth of my past was my husband; I hadn't shared it with anyone else.

My mom lived too far away for us to talk in person, and I knew I couldn't do it over the phone. So I mustered my courage and wrote her a letter. It was a painful letter to write. My only solace was that I wouldn't be there when she read it. That was selfish, but thankfully God offered us both grace as we walked through that time. Upon receiving the letter, my mom called me right away. I was relieved when I heard the love in her voice—love that seemed even deeper because of my openness and honesty.

What a shame that it had to be this confession that brought us closer together. But I'm grateful that God orchestrated it, or Mom and I would still be emotionally distant from each other.

I lost many years to a lie. You know the lie…the one that insists that no one will accept you once they know the truth. But I'm happy to say that I've evicted that falsehood from my mind.

The grace God demonstrated through my mom gave me the courage to tell my story again. And again. First to a friend, and then, unexpectedly, to a room full of women at my Bible study. I was still nervous about what others would think, but each time God offered me grace and love through the ones with whom He told me to share. In fact, my openness prompted many of the other women to share similar stories. God knew what He was doing.

With each woman I told, I felt the burden lift a little more. I was finding it easier to be more open and transparent with people. It was very freeing to be completely honest for the first time in my life.

Then one day I told Gaylyn, the woman who directs the postabortion Bible study at the Pregnancy Resource Center where I volunteer. I didn't mean to; it kind of slipped out. Gaylyn told me about the postabortion Bible study and encouraged me to attend. Gently cutting her off, I gave her the standard line: "I'm forgiven for that. Thanks anyway, but I'm just fine." Translated, that meant: "I can't talk about it beyond my simple confession, so the thought of dealing with it for several weeks in a Bible study is inconceivable."

I didn't know it yet, but as I began to open up to people, God was working His will in my life. Sharing my secret began to diffuse the power of the secret over me, because I realized I was not alone. People didn't reject me, but offered grace instead.

Then one Saturday I went to our women's Coffee Talk at

church. Even though the program had been offered all year, this was the first time I had attended. No accident. God had orchestrated everything perfectly. On this day a woman shared with the group about her abortion.

I couldn't believe abortion was being discussed in public. In all my forty-six years of church attendance, no one had shared publicly regarding their ugly past, let alone about something as horrific as abortion.

But the test came for me at the end of her talk. She asked us to bow our heads and close our eyes. She wanted to pray for healing for those who had experienced an abortion. I was doing okay so far, but then she asked those who had had an abortion to raise our hands. I couldn't do it. My arm hung heavy at my side. I struggled inside myself during those tense moments, one part wanting to be open and honest, the other filled with shame and fear. Then I heard God's gentle voice. *Barb, if you're really "fine," why can't you even raise your hand?*

That's when I knew that forgiveness, as great as it is, was not enough. I needed healing, too. In that moment, I understood the difference between the two. God had already forgiven me, but He wanted to heal me as well. He was drawing me with His relentless love to a place of total wholeness and freedom from the wounds of my past.

Jesus said in Revelation 21:5, "I am making everything new!" I wanted that—to be thoroughly renewed. I longed to see my past, present, and future in a whole new way. Here and now, God was saying that He was ready to make that true for me.

Yes, I said to Him. Whatever is necessary. Please heal me.

I wasn't bold enough to raise my hand during the prayer time, but afterward Gaylyn was standing at the back of the room. I went to her and said, "I was wrong. I'm not fine. I'm ready to join the postabortion study."

God had already given me a glimpse ahead, so I knew that the journey was going to be painful. Why was I ready now and not before? Because this time I was truly desperate. I was hungry for something better than the emotional prison I still inhabited. God's Spirit within me gave me hope that things could be different. I didn't have to live like this anymore.

In some ways it was like surrendering to elective knee-replacement surgery. Keeping the old knee might mean pain with every step, as well as limited lifetime activities. But at least then I knew what tomorrow would bring and how I would feel every day.

On the other hand, submitting to surgery would mean excruciating pain and extended time off for recovery, all for an unknown future. Would my new heart really be pain free? After all the effort—bringing up old issues, choosing to feel the hurt, working through the memories and shame—would my new life feel any different? What if I endured the process for nothing?

Hanging on to old ways is familiar and comfortable. I'd learned to successfully adjust and cope with my pain—or so I thought. But finally God pushed me across the threshold.

The Good in Pain

Are you tempted to stay with your old ways, as I was, rather than to venture into the unknown, even if the unknown is the truth?

One of the most enlightening books I've ever read is *How People Grow*[1] by Drs. Henry Cloud and John Townsend. In it, the authors spend a whole chapter on the absolute necessity of embracing pain in order to heal. They describe two kinds of pain—bad pain and good pain. They explain that the "bad pain comes from repeating old patterns" that help us avoid "the suffering it would take to change them," and that "bad pain is basically wasted pain. It is the pain we go through to avoid the good pain of growth that comes from pushing through." The bad pain is really our way of self medicating the pain instead of dealing with it.

In contrast, good pain leads to healing. When we expose our pain, it hurts. But it allows God to shine His light of truth on every aspect of our lives, and then true healing occurs. This vulnerability is difficult because our natural tendency is to avoid pain. But avoidance blocks healing.

In 1 Peter 4:1–2, Peter talks about suffering. "Therefore, since Christ suffered in his body, arm yourselves also with the same attitude, because he who has suffered in his body is done with sin. As a result, he does not live the rest of his earthly life for evil human desires, but rather for the will of God." Christ's attitude was to embrace suffering—not avoid it. He knew the redemptive quality of suffering and was willing to endure it completely and thoroughly so that we would know its healing power.

Watching the movie *The Passion of the Christ* was an intense, emotional experience for me from beginning to end. But one scene continues to play over and over in my mind. It was when Christ was being beaten, His hands tied to the stake. Utterly exhausted and traumatized, His blood-soaked body collapsed to the ground.

The Romans never intentionally beat someone to death—just to death's door. Jesus could have stayed on the ground, and the beatings would have stopped. What He did next will forever be ingrained on my heart and mind.

He got up. He pulled Himself to His feet and stood as tall as His broken, bleeding body and His shackles would allow, knowing full well that the soldiers would have to continue whipping Him. The guards were stunned. So was I. Reluctantly, the soldiers resumed the most brutal beating I've ever witnessed.

What made Him do that? I would've stayed on the ground. But He didn't. He is for us an incredible model of courage in the face of necessary suffering. Christ purposefully embraced all of the pain required to bring about our complete healing.

According to 1 Peter 4:1, above, when we embrace all of our good pain, then we are done with sin. It no longer can keep its hold on us. We never have to deal with that particular sin again.

Does that sound like freedom to you?

The moment at which we voluntarily opt for "heart surgery" is the moment of *repentance*. That's when we offer God our sin and our pain, and we *confess* (agree with God about) the mess we're in and our need for His help. This is the step that softens and opens our hearts to receive God's forgiveness, love, and truth.

Submitting to the good pain allows forgiveness, love, and truth to eradicate the bad pain that has invaded our souls, so that we can be healed. You can't have healing without good pain, especially with sexual sin.

Unique Sin, Unique Injury

Beth Moore, in *When Godly People Do Ungodly Things*,[2] writes about forgiveness and healing from sexual sin:

Stealing, like all sin, is serious and carries lasting consequences of violating God's law. Yet if I stole money and then changed my mind and dumped it in the garbage, in some respects I could walk away without taking the sin with me. However, if I commit sexual sin, I have a much harder time dumping the garbage. Why? Because spiritually speaking, it got on me somehow. The sin was against my own body and wields a much stronger staying power. Sexual sin can be dumped, all right, but not in a garbage bin. Only Christ through the power of His cross can peel off the adhesive effects of sexual sin.... *The sin is forgiven the moment the person repents, but healing from the ramifications can take longer* (emphasis mine).... Beloved, we must learn to trust God with our sexuality.... Surely it's more than coincidental that Satan is having his greatest field day over the very dimension of our lives that we are most reluctant to bring before God for help, healing and wholeness.

Why doesn't sexual sin have the same effect as stealing or lying? Why is it that after I've gossiped or cheated someone, and then asked for forgiveness, I can let it go? When I think of that sin again, I don't have an ongoing sense of unforgiveness or shame.

What is it about sexual sin that attaches itself to us so completely that even after asking for forgiveness a million times, we never feel forgiven, even decades later?

Let me share with you what I believe God has revealed to me about this very complex issue of sexual sin, sexual bonding, and the shame and remorse we feel.

We've already seen how sexual bonding causes a long-term attachment to the other person, to that experience, and to all the circumstances surrounding that relationship—whether the experience was pleasant or painful. But what is it about sexual sin that requires healing as well as forgiveness?

To answer that question, God drew my attention to two verses. First Corinthians 6:18 explains that when we sin sexually, we sin against our own bodies, as we saw in chapter 2. And again, 1 Thessalonians 4:3–6 says, "It is God's will that you should be sanctified: that you should avoid sexual immorality; that each of you should learn to control his own body in a way that is holy and honorable, not in passionate lust like the heathen, who do not know God; *and that in this matter no one should wrong his brother or take advantage of him*" (emphasis mine).

Even though I'd read those verses many times, God opened my eyes to see something I hadn't realized before. When God says we sin against ourselves, He means that *everything sexually wrong that we've done to the other person, we've also done to ourselves*. The Thessalonians passage says that when we use someone sexually outside marriage, we are wronging them and taking advantage of them. In some translations (KJV, NASB) the word for "taking advantage" is translated "defrauding." To defraud is to rob someone of something.

Of what is someone robbed in sexual sin?

Ultimately, they are robbed of a special God-given gift that is meant for one person—their future spouse. But additionally, they are robbed of the true love and intimacy that goes along with that gift in marriage. They're robbed of intimacy with God, of human dignity, of trust and the ability to bond with one person for life. They're robbed of saving sexual desire and arousal for their future spouse. They're robbed of an unattached and pure mind, body, soul, and spirit.

And if we go a step further, we realize that the person's future spouse is robbed of all of these treasures as well.

Why does sexual sin hurt us so much? Because the very first time we engage in sex outside God's plan—in that precise moment our eyes are opened. Sex is no longer a curious mystery or a desire yet to be satisfied. In an instant our hearts know that this is indeed something special, something holy, and something divine.

And something lost.

We've taken a valuable treasure from the other person. *And we've also robbed ourselves.* We now know that we've cheated ourselves of something that can never be replaced, and the remorse, the regret, the pain settle deep into our souls.

Avoiding the Doctor

How could something that God created as holy, pure, and precious become so shameful, cheap, and misused? Satan took what God designed for our good and used it against us. Because sex involves the whole person—spirit, emotions, mind, and body—its abuse causes comprehensive damage. But the greatest impact of sexual sin is relational.

What a shrewd plan. What better way to keep people from drawing closer to God than to keep them from trusting people? And if I can't trust you, whom I see, then I most certainly can't trust a God that I can't see.

What's our immediate reaction to pain? We try to get rid of it. And so we hide it away, rationalizing why we shouldn't feel this way, shutting out the thoughts of what we've done.

Our strategy for survival is to bury the memories and feelings deep in the hidden places of our soul, so that no one can ever know. Even God. Then we won't have to feel.

That, my friend, is the destructive reality of bad pain. It keeps us in a continual state of avoidance—avoiding God, avoiding healthy relationships, avoiding change, and avoiding wholeness. Dr. Dan Allender says it best in his book *The Wounded Heart:*[3] "Hiding the past always involves denial; denial of the past is always a denial of God." He says that embracing the pain of the past is a "labor eminently worthy of every believer to reclaim the parts of one's soul that remain untilled and unproductive for bearing fruit. And the denial of the past hinders this work of reclamation."

I lead a Bible study for women who've experienced sexual damage in their pasts and are longing for healing. At the first meeting, we handed out guidelines to help group members prepare an outline of their stories so they could share the stories the following week. When I called one participant, named Mary, to see how her preparations were going, she said an interesting thing to me: "I was trying to decide whether I should write my story down ahead of time, or just wing it. But then I realized I was avoiding writing it down because in order to do that I would have to think about it. And I can't think about it without feeling the pain all over again."

She went on to share how God had shown her that, in order to experience the healing she desired, she'd have to embrace the memories, the pain, and the shame. That meant she needed to write it down, to see it in black and white, to acknowledge that it actually happened.

When I called Alice, another member of the group, she

surprised me with her statement. "I am so glad we are doing this," she said. "This is the first time I have ever thought about some of this stuff, let alone written it down. I am now able to see how my past has influenced some of my choices and why I'm where I am today."

For both of these women, the process of exposing what had been held in secret gave God the opportunity to shine His light on their past pain. The result for them was a glimpse of God's plan for healing. One by one, God's truths are revealed, like rays of light burning through the fog. Each revealed truth breaks the hold of the lie it exposes. Step by step, truth brings freedom, and freedom brings healing and wholeness.

Picture a puppet with all its body parts attached by strings to a single stick. One person controls the puppet's every movement by maneuvering the stick. Like a puppet master, the enemy uses lies we hold in secret to control our thoughts, attitudes, choices, emotions, and reactions. God showed me that I was a puppet, allowing pain, shame, and lies to control me. As He began to release me from the lies, I envisioned God cutting my strings one by one until I was no longer attached to the controlling stick. I was free! Free to be who God created me to be. Free to become all that He purposed for me. Free to experience the abundant life that He promised and that I longed for.

Many times in the Gospels, Jesus provided healing and forgiveness. My favorite story is the healing of the bleeding woman (Luke 8:42–48). This poor woman had been subject to bleeding for twelve years. She suffered a great deal under the care of many doctors and spent all she had. Yet instead of getting better, she got worse. That's not all. In her culture the bleeding condition made her unclean, and therefore untouchable. Because of it, she was condemned to a lonely life of shame and pain.

But she heard that Jesus was coming, and she said to herself, "If I just touch his clothes, I will be healed."

The moment she touched Jesus' garment, she was healed. But then the story gets interesting. She tried to retreat back into the crowd and go away unnoticed. But Jesus didn't allow her to. Immediately, He turned and asked, "Who touched me?"

Of course, Jesus already knew who had touched Him. So why insist that she come forward and expose herself to Him and all the people? Why was that so important? How was it going to help her?

First of all, her initial healing had only been physical. Jesus also wanted to forgive her sins and heal her spiritually. This is what I love about God. He always wants to exceed our expectations, not just meet them. Her expectations were for physical healing, but Jesus exceeded that by providing her not only with healing here and now, but also with forgiveness of sin for an eternal life free from suffering.

Second, exposing herself made the experience *real* in her memory. Later, when she was alone, the enemy would try to convince her that it had never happened, that she'd only imagined it. But now she would have forever etched in her memory the sound of His voice, the touch of His hand, and the gentle look of love in His eyes as He pronounced her healed and forgiven. The enemy had just been defeated. The bonds to her past were broken, and no one would ever be able to convince her otherwise.

Not now.

And third, by her public exposure, she came to know Jesus in a whole new way. She already knew He was a miracle worker, but she didn't know that He was compassionate, loving, and forgiving. The passage says she came and fell at His feet, trembling with fear. What was she afraid of? Maybe she feared the hardest thing of all—humbling herself and coming forward. I hear it from people all the time. "Oh, I know I'm forgiven, but I can't really tell anyone, because I'm kind of a private person."

I can relate to this woman. I was afraid that people would reject me, would cast their judgmental stones at me, would deem me unworthy of their respect and love.

But I think she was also afraid of Jesus. Maybe, once He realized how unworthy she really was, He would be angry with her and take His power and healing back. Or even worse, maybe He'd punish her. Have you ever been afraid that if you really own up to what you've done, God would reward you with even greater consequences? I was. That thought kept me from drawing closer to God even when I knew He was calling me. *Maybe if I can just forget it, put it out of my mind, it will all go away and I'll never have to deal with it,* I thought.

Trying to hide from God didn't work for this woman. It didn't work for me. And it won't work for you.

Only reaching out to God works. And every time we do, His great love and compassion compels Him to heal and forgive us completely. That means coming humbly before Him, falling at His feet, and giving Him permission to do whatever it takes. Even if you come trembling with fear.

Hurting Toward Healing

Are you that desperate yet? Do you wholeheartedly want God to make a change in your life?

I did. It took a long time. But I finally realized that the pain I was living with had to be greater than the pain of walking this journey with God. I tried everything else—hiding, controlling, performing—and none of it worked. I was desperate for something more. More from life, more from Jesus, more love, more hope. More of everything good. I wanted this abundant life that God was offering, which I certainly wasn't living.

I signed up for that postabortion Bible study. Following through on the commitment was the hardest thing I've ever done. (I'll share more about that in the next chapter.)

I'll be honest: The process of ongoing self-exposure was painful. Gut-wrenching, raw anguish shredded my emotions and turned me into a weeping mess many times.

This may sound odd, but this torment was extremely healing at the same time. As I worked through each issue with God, He removed the hold that the related emotions and thoughts had over me.

One issue would dissolve, only to be replaced by the next one, weighing down on me anew.

But hope grew. With each resolved struggle, with each surgically removed cancer, a flood of peace, joy, and love came in to replace it. Piece by piece, issue by issue, God used the good pain to gently clean out all the bad pain.

It was extremely hard work, but I felt God's encouragement all the way, and I knew that He was rewarding my efforts. I began to change from the inside out. I stopped identifying myself with my past. I began to identify myself with what God had done and was continuing to do in me. My anxiety and depression subsided, my energy increased, and I began to feel better about myself. I became more decisive, more confident, more humble, and more compassionate toward others.

In an earlier chapter, I described how I began to feel again, to actually experience emotions like joy and sadness. It was so cleansing to cry. As I drained myself of tears, I felt God replace them with joy, gratitude, and love.

It's been a little over a year now since I finished the postabortion Bible study, and God continues to complete His perfect healing work in me. Through a recent incident, He revealed that He has accomplished significant healing in my life. I was sitting at a conference, listening to a woman discuss abortion and postabortion work for ninety minutes. I sat there with amazing calm as this woman tearfully described her work with women before and after their abortions.

I felt no shame.

This was the first time I was ever able to sit through a discussion about abortion without the overwhelming urge to run out of the room. It was a delicious moment of victory for me. But it wasn't my victory alone. I was overcome with gratitude for the One who had accomplished this amazing miracle in me.

I did have that talk with my kids. It was the hardest thing I've ever done. Do you know what finally gave me the courage? I replaced my story with God's story. My life is all about what God has done. I've shifted my focus onto Him, so that He gets the glory. I wanted my kids to know that God was the star, the hero. And without Him I was nothing.

That First Risky Step

You are not the only one who will benefit from your healing. God is calling us all into complete wholeness so that He can use us in the lives of people around us. That doesn't mean you'll end up speaking and writing on the topic, as I have. But you can be sure that somehow He will take what was evil and turn it toward good, both for you and for others.

I've said before that your journey may not look like mine, because your past is different from mine. Indulge me as I say it again. God may not call you to tell your kids. I don't know; only He does.

But I do know one thing. Imagine me calling on you today to raise your hand, to expose your deep dark secret. If in that scenario your shame would bind that hand to your side—then I know you're the one God is calling.

He's calling you out as He called the bleeding woman.

He wants you to have the complete package, both for-giveness and healing.

And healing starts with exposure to the light.

How desperate are you?

Part Two

A HEART **SET FREE**

A HEART SET FREE
A HEART SET FREE
A HEART SET FREE
A HEART SET FREE
A HEART SET FREE
A HEART SET FREE
A HEART SET FREE
A HEART SET FREE

NEW HEART

Breaking the Bonds of Sex

It didn't happen overnight. It didn't happen in a month, or even six months. This journey on which God continues to lead me began four years ago.

In the first chapter, I mentioned our move to California. God had my undivided attention for the first time in over twenty-five years, and I didn't like it. God pursued, convicted, and spoke to me every day as I wandered around my new home cleaning and unpacking. It was a bittersweet experience. It was sweet because God provided a glimpse into the life that He was making available to me—a life brimming with more of Him. It was also bitter because He showed me that I first had to remove some painful, ugly obstacles.

I was afraid that others might learn of my past, so at first I declined God's offer. Thankfully, God doesn't take no for an answer. He continued to pursue me and to prove that He was trustworthy. The more I discovered about His character, the softer my heart became.

I want to share the process through which God gently led me, my journey with Him along this amazing path to healing. Although your journey will differ from mine, the basic steps are the same.

First, it started with surrender, which allowed God to break down the wall of pride in my life.

This led to the second step, true repentance, and the third, understanding the root cause of my sin.

Fourth came obedience—trusting God enough to do whatever He required for complete healing. (Obedience is what allows me to continue experiencing the healing power of Christ in my life today.)

And the final step was to write a sexual history list and to pray through it, asking God to break the sexual bonds I had created with each of my past partners. I haven't finished step five; it's an ongoing process for me. I've created multiple lists as God continues to reveal more from those years. It's painful, but God is gracious to give me only what I can handle. With Him leading the way, it's easy to follow.

As you read my story, ask God to examine your heart in preparation for each stage. He will guide you each step of the way.

STEPS TO BREAKING FREE

Step One: Surrender

Submit. Surrender. Relinquish. They all mean the same thing— to give up control to someone else. This goes against our every self-protective instinct, yet God says surrender is the only way we will ever experience life in Him.

In all four gospels, Jesus repeats this formula: "Whoever

wants to save his life will lose it, but whoever loses his life for me will save it" (Luke 9:24). The only way to have life is to give up total control of mind, heart, soul, will, and body.

Over the years, I had surrendered often with my lips, but never with my heart and soul. I'd give God parts of myself that I couldn't control anyway, where I had nothing to lose. All the other parts I kept tightly in my grasp.

But God is patient. He wants us to surrender everything to Him of our own free will. We must *choose* to surrender. We must consciously, willingly come before God waving our white flags, laying down our lives, and trusting that He is better at controlling things than we are.

This is where my journey began, at the all-important door of surrender. By stepping through it, I opened my heart, and God took over. He taught me how to pray and how to obey. Once He stepped into action, I never looked back. And I've never been the same.

The verse that helped me in my prayer of surrender was Psalm 25:4–5: "Show me your ways, O LORD, teach me your paths; guide me in your truth and teach me, for you are God my Savior, and my hope is in you all day long."

The requests, "show me...teach me...guide me," are expressions of humility and dependence—as a child to a teacher or parent—for instruction and direction. By asking God to show us His ways, His plans, His truth, we relinquish our own plans, ways, and what we think is truth. We then replace them with God's. This is surrender.

This step broke down the wall I had erected, without realizing it, around my heart. I built the wall in an effort to protect myself from further wounding. But by hiding behind the wall, I was hurting others in my life.

Surrender was the critical first step, but it was only the beginning of all I needed to learn. As God continued to soften my heart and dissolve my barriers, He led me to the next step.

Step Two: True Repentance

In July 2001, I sat in church listening to Pastor Greg Kreiger preach. I don't remember his topic or much else about the message; I only remember one line. He shared that God had led him to pray this simple request: "Lord, break me where I have pride and heal me where I'm broken." That prayer stood out like a neon sign, and I knew immediately that God wanted me to make it my own.

The next morning in my quiet time I prayed, "Lord, break me where I have pride and heal me where I'm broken."

I didn't know what to expect. I didn't think I had a problem with pride. Actually, I thought my problem was just the opposite—a low sense of self-worth.

It didn't take God long to answer. Within a few days, He revealed to me that my low sense of self-worth was itself prideful. How so? My inferiority complex caused me to focus on myself and not on God. Pride is anything that keeps us focused on ourselves, not on Him. My pride didn't elevate me, but rather *insulated* me. Because I was internally focused, I wasn't able to focus on others. God couldn't use me to serve Him and the people in my life. How was God going to use me to comfort people if I couldn't take the focus off myself?

To this borrowed prayer for brokenness and healing I added David's prayer from Psalm 139:23–24: "Search me, O God, and know my heart; test me and know my anxious thoughts. See if there is any offensive way in me, and lead me in the way everlasting."

Anxiety was part of my everyday life. I knew it well. So when I found a verse that talked about an anxious heart, I paid attention. When I clothe myself in worry, I withdraw from others, and they feel rejected and hurt by my neglect. God revealed to me that my anxiousness was sin, because it was an unwillingness to trust Him. My anxiousness about the wrongs and damage of my past caused me to hurt everyone in my life.

It was time to trust God with the secrets.

It was time to give Him my broken heart. To give Him the mess of my past. To give Him the despair for my future.

And God was indeed faithful. Just as He promises in Isaiah 61:1–3, He took my offering of ashes and replaced it with a crown of beauty. He took my spirit of despair and replaced it with a garment of praise. And He took the scattered, wounded pieces of my heart and bound them together again so that I could heal.

The greatest benefit of being broken is that it makes us teachable. It softens heart, will, and attitude so that we are able to learn and grow. It realigns our direction, our purpose. Instead of stalling out, we progress. Rather than stagnating, we flourish.

A proud heart keeps running into the same obstacles, and is defeated again and again. But a broken heart victoriously conquers new ground daily.

Step Three: Understanding the Root of Sin

One of the most impactful insights I've gained has to do with the real cause of my sin. As I focused on my sexual sin, the divorce, the abortion, I couldn't understand how I was capable of such wrongs, especially as a Christian. This was the greatest obstacle keeping me from letting God have my past. I couldn't reconcile the fact that even though I knew the truth I had made such immoral choices.

The problem was that I had been focusing on the sin itself. God wanted me to see what was at the *root* of my sin.

The root, I learned, was a hardened heart towards God.

I have studied great men and women of God in the Bible. And I've come to realize that whenever God approached them about their outward sins, He first revealed to them that their actions were only symptoms of their heart condition—some form of hardening against Him. Once we turn our hearts away from God and stop listening to His voice, we are capable of anything. God hasn't established a hierarchy of sins, because there is no limit to the depth of evil to which a hardened heart can stoop.

One way a hardened heart manifests itself is by independence. In Jeremiah 2:13 God said of Israel, "My people have committed two sins: they have forsaken me, the spring of living water, and have dug their own cisterns, broken cisterns that cannot hold water." Those two sins—turning away from God and putting our trust and confidence in someone or something else—are at the root of all sin. Whenever we turn our backs on what God wants and go our own way, we place ourselves at the mercy of our own deceitful hearts and Satan's schemes. And then no sin is out of reach.

I find the contrasting pictures in this verse amazing. Following God's way is like having access to a living spring with a limitless fresh supply at our disposal for eternity. The result is an abundant life, overflowing with love, joy, peace, and hope.

Neighbors at our cottage in Northern Ontario discovered an aquifer deep in the ground by their cottage and dug a well.

An aquifer is a spring under the ground that continues to flow until it reaches a body of water. When you dig a well into the aquifer, you capture the water as it flows by. Whenever water is pumped out of the well, fresh water flows into the well to replace it. Because of the well, our neighbors have a continuous supply of fresh spring water every time they turn on their tap.

But going our own way is like digging our own cisterns. The first problem with this is that a cistern is not a source of water; it is a storage place for water from another source. Building an empty cistern gives you...an empty cistern, if you aren't able to collect water into it from somewhere else. What is more, God says that our independently constructed cisterns are broken and useless. Whatever water might chance to flow into them flows right back out. We end up empty and dry.

Once I realized that my deepest sin was not the abortion, but my independent, hardened heart, I experienced true repentance. I use the term "true" because I think my previous repentance had been selfish. I had been sorry for what I'd done, but only because of the ways that it had impacted me. I was tired of the feelings of shame, regret, and pain, and I wanted to be rid of them. I was *less* committed to getting rid of their real cause. My repeated confessions were inspired by a desire for reconciliation with God, but only so that *I* would feel better.

When I understood the root of my sin, I became overwhelmed by what I had done to *Him*. I had hurt God. My hardened heart was an offense against Him.

It was also an offense against the baby to whom I had denied life. I had hurt her more than I had hurt myself. For the first time, I stopped feeling sorry for myself and felt real heart-wrenching pain for God, my baby, and others I'd harmed.

In 2 Corinthians 7:10, Paul talks about two kinds of sorrow: "Godly sorrow brings repentance that leads to salvation and leaves no regret, but worldly sorrow brings death." I realized that up until that point my sorrow had been worldly. How did I know? Because Paul's implication is that worldly sorry brings regret, and though I'd asked God to forgive me many times, I still felt regret. But when I experienced true godly sorrow, my shame and regret were gone.

Drs. Henry Cloud and John Townsend clarify the difference between godly and worldly sorrow in *How People Grow.*[1] "Worldly sorrow can keep us from feeling forgiven.... [It] is not based in love, but on oneself and one's own badness.... On the other hand, godly sorrow focuses on the offended party. The Bible says we should not feel guilty, but we should feel sorry. There is a big difference. Godly sorrow ends up in repentance. When we realize we are hurting someone we love, we change.... But guilt [or worldly sorrow] actually causes sin to increase.... It only makes people rebel more."

God demonstrated this for me while I was praying to break my sexual bonds. I made a list of everyone with whom I had been sexually promiscuous and, starting at the top, asked God to break the bonds. (More on this later.) Although none of my experiences could be considered sexual abuse, I felt as much victim as initiator in most of those situations. Many of the men had exerted subtle pressure on me for sex.

As I first began to pray, my mind focused on asking God to forgive them for sins against me. But as I proceeded down my list, something amazing happened. God began to show me the offenses I had committed against these men. I had robbed them as much as they had robbed me. God made it clear that I had used these men in my search for love and acceptance instead of going to Him. I hadn't really loved any of them. I had no intention of marrying them. Yet I had been willing to use them to fulfill my need.

I changed my prayer focus from what they had done to me to what I had done to them. In this way, I again experienced true repentance. I was taking responsibility that I had previously denied.

For the first time I had no regret. Godly sorrow finally broke the hold my past had on me.

Step Four: Obedience

"Because I said so."

That was my mother's usual justification when I challenged her commands. It didn't go over very well with my sometimes-rebellious heart. I wanted a reason…a "good enough" reason…a better reason than "just because." She didn't often have one. Or if she did, she was seldom forthcoming with it.

As a Baptist girl growing up, I was taught that God also had a lot of bizarre, little-understood rules. My spiritual to-don't list was longer than my to-do list. And my mother's justification for all of these was just as enlightening as her justification for her own rules—"because *God* said so." God appeared to be just as unreasonable about providing "good enough" answers as my mom.

When I became a mom, I determined to back up God's and my commands with a little more substance than "because we said so." But experience taught me what I hadn't understood as a child. As a mother of four, I now appreciate how children's demands can beat you down until, stripped of compassion and patience, you quiet them with the because-I-said-so line. I've been there. And I now know that what my mom really meant was, *Trust me, because I love you and I know what's best for you.* She hadn't been as unreasonable as I had thought.

It took me a long time to realize that God's Word wasn't one big "just because." Everything about His name, His character, and His Word echoes the sentiment: *Trust me, because I love you and I know what's best for you.* And even when He doesn't explain His commands, He leaves me with no doubt about His love for me.

I don't know about you, but I warm up to compassion much more than to the near-meaningless "just because." I bristle and withdraw from dictatorship, but I am drawn to someone who loves me and cares about my best.

Are you willing to obey God fully, even if you don't understand the "because" of His commands? Satan's most effective tactic is to cast doubt on God's love. Then we keep our hearts distant from Him, and go through only the minimal, understandable, "safe" motions that we think will satisfy Him. Satan deceives us into believing that as long as we go to church, read our Bibles, and pray, it's enough. He knows that if he can keep Christians from completely trusting God—if he can keep us from obeying when we don't understand—we will never truly experience God's life-changing power. We will be weak and ineffective. Powerless Christians provide no threat to Satan's plan to turn the world against God.

Beth Moore, in *When Godly People Do Ungodly Things,*[2] says that this is the difference between, on the one hand, letting the Word of God merely get *to* us and, on the other hand, letting it get *in and through* us. She writes, "Many of those who get a steady diet of the Word of God don't deliberately receive it (by applying it) through and through." First Thessalonians 5:23–24 states that God wants to sanctify us through and through—to completely permeate our spirits, souls, and bodies with His cleansing power and presence. Moore emphasizes that we can read the Bible every day, but if we don't meditate on it throughout the day—allowing it to penetrate into our depths, and then letting it emerge out into action—we won't change.

Real obedience from a God-drenched heart is the difference. I spent years reading the Bible, attending church, and praying occasionally, but I only allowed His Word to touch the surface. Deciding to trust God, and then obeying what He truly asked of me—not just putting on an external show—changed my life and my relationship with Him.

It wasn't easy. Not only were some of His commands difficult, but they often didn't make sense at the time. I discovered that God didn't fit inside the box I had built for Him. He is a radical, on-the-edge kind of God. But the proof was in the doing. Each time I obeyed in spite of my fear, I liked the result and was encouraged to say yes the next time.

One of the first things God asked me to do was to return some money that had been given to me. Twenty years before, I had taught at a Christian school in Virginia. At the time the school paid heads of household one thousand dollars more annually than someone whose income was the second in their home. Since I was married, I was not eligible for the extra amount, which was okay with me. About two years after we moved back to Canada, I received a check in the mail from the school. Apparently someone had sued them for pay discrimination. The school lost the lawsuit and sent checks to anyone who hadn't received the additional money—one thousand dollars multiplied by the number of years worked.

I fully intended to return the money. I had understood and agreed to the "discriminatory" arrangement, and I didn't feel entitled to this money. I also knew how this settlement would hurt the school financially. I opened an American bank account and deposited the money, planning to write a check back to the school.

Twenty years later I still hadn't returned the money. Each year we traveled to California to visit my husband's family, and we found it more economical to withdraw some of the school money than to lose precious pennies on the exchange rate. Eventually the money was gone. Along with my intention to return it.

God couldn't have chosen worse timing to start reminding me about it. My husband's job wasn't working out as we'd anticipated. His company was unable to procure the investment capital they had expected, and Eric's pay was cut in half. We ended up living on our savings. Paying back a large sum of money at this time was unthinkable.

I made excuses. I couldn't remember the amount of the original check. I wasn't even sure if the school still existed. These allowed me to put off my God-given responsibility for a while.

I'll never forget the day I sat in my prayer closet asking God to search my heart and show me my sin. God said, *Barb, stop talking! I am not impressed with your intentions. What I want is action. Go and write that check. Then we'll talk.*

He got my attention. Immediately I went to the computer,

and within seconds, not only was the name of the school staring me in the face, but also the pastor of the associated church and the school board members.

"Okay, God," I said, "You win. Now I just need to know the amount."

Once again God came through. I remembered that the school had sent me $1,300.

Only one obstacle remained. I couldn't just send $1,300 without my husband's blessing, especially given our financial struggle. I told God that if this was His will, He would have to make Eric agree.

Eric said yes. With that, God had removed my last excuse and made it impossible to say no with a clear conscience. Within an hour of receiving God's rebuke and leaving my prayer closet, I had written the letter, signed the check, and stamped the envelope. I sensed a warm reception as I reentered my closet to resume my meeting with God that morning. I knew that my faith and obedience had pleased Him. It was an incredible experience.

I didn't expect anything in return for this step of obedience—nothing more than the blessing of His pleasure and presence. But God loves to exceed our expectations; He delights in surprising and blessing us. Less than one month later, God returned every penny from unexpected sources. Yes, all $1,300! In addition, I received letters from the high school principal, the elementary principal, the pastor of the church, and a board member. They were overwhelmed with God's goodness to them through my obedience. Even though the names of four humans are at the bottoms of those letters, I know they were love letters from God. I've kept every one of them.

I experienced God in a whole new way that day. I discovered a God who would ask me to do something that many people would consider strange, just so that He could bless me and I could know Him better. The whole episode whetted my appetite for the next assignment, through which I could further explore the depths of this incredible God I was getting to know and learning to love.

God soon gave me more practice at this new "obedience" thing. Small tasks. Forgiving others, reconciling damaged relationships, apologizing, learning to pray for and love some unlovable people in my life.

He was preparing me for the biggie—exposing my secrets. Thank goodness He didn't spring that one on me before I had experienced plenty of His goodness. If He had, I would have concluded that nothing was worth that kind of vulnerability.

I've shared with you how God led me to open up about my past with my mother, my friends, and my children. Since those early disclosures, He's asked me to share my story with thousands of strangers on radio, at women's conferences, and now in this book. I can now obey to this extent because I experienced His faithfulness during earlier stages of my growth. I've learned that when God asks something of me, the blessings I receive for my obedience will make the often-painful follow-through a distant memory.

My life is now characterized by humility, surrender, and obedience. These are the disciplines of my walk with God. Every day is an incredible adventure as God leads me further down this road toward knowing Him. The more I travel, the farther I want to go. Sometimes I find God slowing me down because my eagerness makes me impatient. He knows that I can't grow up overnight, so He guides my growth at a slow, steady pace. He wants me to grasp His lessons the first time, rather than having to relearn them later. I trust Him with the content of the lessons and the pace of the growth of this often-faltering student.

One of my life verses is Isaiah 66:2, where God says, "This is the one I esteem: he who is humble and contrite in spirit [heart], and trembles at my word." The humble, surrendered, obedient heart is the one that pleases Him. Those qualities are opposite from what we would otherwise value. Our natural tendency is to strive independently and pridefully for sinlessness, service, and sacrifice—all good values, except that we often try to perform them as outward signs to *earn* God's acceptance. But God—the One who sees the hearts of men—says that it's the condition of the heart, not just outward practice, that pleases Him most.

Knowing God and pleasing Him are the two greatest desires of my heart. I'm so grateful that God removes the complexities of the performance-oriented life and makes it possible for me to achieve my heart's desires through simple, humble surrender and obedience.

Step Five: The Prayer to Break Sexual Bonds

The next step toward healing that God showed me was praying to break sexual bonds. I don't think the specific words matter as much as the faith with which you utter them. You must believe that God will break the ties you have made, freeing you to give yourself wholly to Him.

First, you need to prayerfully write out a sexual history list. Take some quiet, undistracted time with God to allow Him the opportunity to show you the names, faces, and events of your sexual past. You may have forgotten some of these, or purposely denied them and removed them from your memory because of pain and shame. Allow Him to remind you of all the bonds created in your past. You need God's healing for each one.

At the least, your list will include everyone with whom you've had sex outside of marriage. It may also include those with whom you've had emotional, fantasizing affairs, and those with whom you did everything short of intercourse. Some of the faces God reveals may be fake people—those on the Internet, in a magazine, on the phone, or in a video—those with whom you became bonded through pornographic sex. Your list will include faces of people who used you for their pleasure, against your will, through rape or sexual abuse. Include one-night stands as well as long, committed relationships—people you were too drunk to know and people you knew very well. Your list should include those you married and divorced, and the partners you just lived with. It should even include your current spouse if you had sex with him or her before you were married.

Write down everything God shows you. If you don't know a name, write down where you were, what you did—anything you remember. This is an important part of the process. Putting our past actions down in black and white takes away the deception that they never happened.

And this is where most people get stuck.

"The list is too long," they lament. "I'll never get through it all."

Or, "God will never forgive all this."

Stuck is exactly the way the enemy wants you to stay—stuck on the other side of the door to healing. Opening that door and walking through will be the hardest part of your journey.

But give God a chance. He already knows the secrets of your heart that need to be revealed. He knows how much time you'll need for healing. He knows how much courage you'll need in order to face what you must see. And He'll provide everything you need. He'll stand beside you the whole way.

Now, once God has revealed your list and you've written it down—that's when you're ready to ask Him to give you His eyes, so that you can see your sin the way that He sees it. I prayed for this perspective when I worked through my list. And God answered. Once He showed me His view of my sin, my attitude and intensity in prayer changed—became other-focused, rather than self-focused—and I experienced true repentance. Seeing my sin through God's eyes played an important role in breaking my invisible bonds.

In chapter 5, I referred to 1 Peter 4:1: "He who has suffered in his body is done with sin." Each time I prayed to gain God's perspective on my sin with a particular person, I experienced momentary suffering; I realized the gravity of what I had done. In the intensity of the repentance that followed, I felt God literally cut the cord that held me to that person. In my mind, I saw God take a large pair of heavenly scissors and sever the ties. I saw the cord fall away, and with it the person on the other end. I felt a sense of lightness and release.

With each name on my list, I prayed that God would restore to me all the torn-off parts of myself that I had given to the other person, and that He would remove from within me all the shreds of the other person that had become attached to me. With each prayer of release, I felt more and more wholeness within myself, and less and less invisible attachment to my past sexual partners.

God has performed this miracle over and over inside me since then. And as He brings to mind more faces and sinful circumstances from time to time, I expect Him to continue performing it many more times.

He wants to do the same work in you.

Since step five includes several mini-steps, let me summarize it for you here:

1. Ask God to bring to mind everyone with whom you've had sexual contact—voluntarily or involuntarily. Wait quietly, allowing God to bring names, faces, or events to memory.

2. Write down each name. If you don't know the name, write a description of the person or event.

3. Ask God to help you see your sin with His eyes.

4. Pray that your heart will be humbled and your spirit contrite, so that you will experience true repentance.

5. Pray the prayer below (or something like it) for each name or incident on your list.

Lord, I ask forgiveness for sinning against You and against my own body. In the name of Jesus Christ, I sever and renounce the bonds I created with _____. In the name of Jesus, I release my heart tie with this person physically, emotionally, and spiritually. I choose by faith to forgive

_____ for the violation against me. I also
ask for forgiveness of my violation of him (or her).
Please remove the negative emotional baggage that I
have been carrying around with me, by which I have
been harming others. Restore to me a virgin heart, as
though I had never been with this person, and heal
me completely of the damage this sin has caused my
body, my soul, and my spirit. I accept your forgiveness, and I reject the enemy's attack—his attempts to
fill me with shame associated with this person. I claim
complete healing and restoration in the name of
Jesus. Amen."[3]

If you became bonded through rape or sexual abuse,
omit the prayer asking God to forgive you of your violation
against the other person; you were an innocent victim and had
no intention of violating or defrauding him or her in this man-
ner (see 1 Thessalonians 4:6). But you *do* need to forgive that
person for violating *you*. And you need to ask God to sever the
bonds you have inadvertently created with that person.

How're You Doing?

Okay, time for a quick heart check. How are you feeling
about this exercise?

Did you start but then find it too difficult to continue? If
that's the case, you're not alone. Don't be discouraged if it
takes several tries to complete your list. Part of the healing
process is grieving what you've done and what you've lost.
You may feel sad or depressed. You may be reluctant to
return to your list once you've begun.

Don't despair. Grieving is God's way of allowing us to feel

the pain so that He can comfort and restore us. Be assured that as you grieve the Holy Spirit within is grieving right along with you. We have a compassionate God—one who wants to lift our heavy burdens and place them on Himself. In exchange, He offers comfort, healing, and love. Let Him have your pain. He is trustworthy. You can be confident that He'll reveal whatever you need to see *when* you need to see it—no sooner, no later. He knows the pace that's right for you.

Now, perhaps you've started the exercise, but you don't feel any different, so you're wondering if you did something wrong. That's okay, too. You're probably right on course. Feelings and truth often follow different paths.

Your experience might be like mine. I had been functioning for so long under deceptive life guidelines, and I had for so long been misusing the emotional wiring God gave me, that I didn't immediately recognize my own new inner workings. For a while, I felt like a stranger to myself.

If that's how you feel, let me introduce you to a new person—the *you* that God created you to be. I think you're going to like the new you.

Meanwhile, trust that God is doing His good work inside you, even if you can't detect it by your feelings. And trust that He will soon make clear to you the freeing, healing work He is already performing within you. In fact, you might even begin to experience this difference as you read stories of freedom from others in the next chapter.

Free at Last!

Once you have finished the procedure I've described in step five, only two important tasks remain.

First, burn your list.

And second, memorize Isaiah 43:18–19:

> *"Forget the former things;*
> *do not dwell on the past.*
> *See, I am doing a new thing!*
> *Now it springs up; do you not perceive it?*
> *I am making a way in the desert*
> *and streams in the wasteland."*

Write out this verse. Memorize it. Claim it as your own, until its truth saturates your heart. And recite it next time the enemy tries to rub your face in your past sin.

You are free of the past, and God is about to do something new!

Are you ready?

VIRGIN HEART

Learning to Live Free

Virgin: adj., 1. free of impurity or stain: unsullied, fresh, unspoiled, not altered by human activity.

Virgin heart: n., 1. the central, inmost part of a person who is now free from the impurity and stains of past, sinful human activities.

All the women in my sexual-healing study shared something in common. Something history defining and soul shaping. Everyone in that room had experienced some form of sexual wounding in her past.

I'll never forget the week we related our stories. I heard about painful episodes that I could never have imagined on my own. Each account was different, unique. Many of the ladies had experienced some form of sexual abuse, either perpetrated by family members or in the form of date rape. For most, the sexual damage had led to promiscuous behavior (some while single, some while married), unplanned pregnancies, abortions, and many destructive coping mechanisms, including drug and alcohol abuse.

This was the first time most of the women had shared their stories. And for most it was the hardest thing they had ever done. I was proud of them. Although their words faltered and their eyes filled with tears, they bravely, purposely pressed on, recounting memories they'd spent a lifetime trying to forget. Their courage came from the hope that God would honor their vulnerability and set them free.

Set them free, He did.

Over the course of the study I encouraged the group members to allow God to help them create a sexual history list, as I've described in step five in the preceding chapter. At the end of the study, as we shared what God had done in our lives, it was evident He used this exercise to impact us all.

Margaret found that putting her sexual history list together and then praying through it allowed God to reveal some deep resentment she still held toward people on her list. She acknowledged that God wanted her to work on forgiveness next.

For Linda, the tangible results were slightly delayed. "It didn't happen right away," she began. But in the days after she prayed through her list, God revealed that she had experienced a miracle. "I started to notice that I felt different—lighter, less burdened."

Cindy's healing gave her victory over an emotional affair with which she was struggling in the present. She learned to take her thoughts captive and give them to God. This discipline helped her resist the enemy's temptation to dwell on impure fantasies.

Melanie, married for the second time to the same man,

still felt emotionally tied to another man, with whom she'd had an affair in the interim. Her emotional and physical bond to the affair kept her guarded, so that she withheld herself physically from her husband, even though she had renewed her commitment to him. After she prayed to break this bond, God prompted her to share with her husband secrets that she'd never told him before. Initially she resisted, but when she obeyed, the affair released its hold on her. She was free to love her husband wholeheartedly.

Cathy, a dear friend of mine, said, "I believed in God's forgiveness. I knew in my head that I had forgiveness. I could confidently tell others about God's forgiveness, and know that it was real. But still, the wound in my soul kept me from experiencing God's healing grace and mercy." Cathy had used a variety of coping mechanisms, from drugs and alcohol to more socially acceptable ones, like "saving the world" and performance-oriented religious service. "Even though the world and church patted me on the back for these behaviors, they were simply a way for me to mask the pain and shame I felt inside," she admitted. "All my attempts to ignore my past and do penance didn't work. In fact, I was simply adding to my sins and hurting those I loved the most." Cathy says she is now free from her self-judgment, condemnation, pain, and guilt. God has replaced these with His unconditional love, grace, and mercy.

Anita was overwhelmed by her list. She initially imagined it shorter, but God brought to mind names and faces she wouldn't have remembered on her own. As she prayed down through the list, she found herself sobbing uncontrollably. She had been unaware of the degree of pain she'd endured all these years. She could only handle half of her list during her first prayer session. The experience was exhausting, emotionally draining. "But wonderful at the same time," she said. Not only did she hear God speak to her for the first time in her new life as a believer; she also acknowledged that she could already feel significant healing.

Then came my turn to share.

Better than New

The severing of my sexual bonds was a multifaceted experience.

First, God removed the yoke of shame from around my neck. In Leviticus 26:13, He says, "I broke the bars of your yoke and enabled you to walk with heads held high." What a perfect picture! I knew what it meant to walk with downcast eyes, bearing such a burden of shame that I found it hard to look people in the eye. But now I can hold my head up high. Not arrogantly, but with humble confidence—confidence in the power of God's grace, where all the credit belongs.

Breaking my sexual bonds also freed me to move forward in my marriage, emotionally and physically, now unshackled from my past. Down came the protective wall I had erected around my heart. My protective pride was replaced with a brokenness wrapped in grace, which now helps me to be open instead of secretive, vulnerable instead of defensive, and other-centered instead of self-centered. I can take risks again.

Although I will always have memories of my past sexual partners, the impressions and images are now distant. I used to carry them at the forefront of my mind, but now they are vague and far away. The greatest victory of all is that when they do come to mind, I can remember them without shame.

Gone is the self-condemnation that the memories used to evoke within me.

As I explained to the ladies in my study group, I haven't arrived yet; God is still working on me. But with the healing comes a brokenness that makes my heart available to Him so that He can continue to do His transforming work.

Transformation. That was the word for the day as I watched the rejuvenated faces of these women and listened to their words of hope. I was witnessing a miracle. A whole room full of miracles! No one got up off a bed and walked. No one watched the rising sun through once-sightless eyes. Not a single person stepped unharmed from a blazing furnace.

Yet this miracle, manifested again and again with each story, was as profoundly life-changing as any of those.

It was the miracle of stained, violated hearts transformed into virgin hearts. Hearts once invisibly bound by shame, secrecy, and condemnation now set free. The angels were throwing a party. An Independence Day bigger than the Fourth of July! God was beaming like a proud Papa, while Satan slammed his fist through a wall in defeat.

Another heart set free. And another. And another.

Cows and Children and Birds—Oh My!

How does it feel to be free? What are the characteristics of a virgin heart?

Visualize the picture God paints in Malachi 4:2: "But for you who revere my name, the sun of righteousness will rise with healing in its wings. And you will go out and leap like calves released from the stall."

Can you see the calves leaping as they're released from their cramped quarters? Or if you weren't raised on a farm, imagine instead unbuckling your child from a car seat after several hours. Excitement! Energy! Joy! Freedom! Remove the restraints, and both calves and children know what to do. They run, they leap, they dance! *Yippee! I'm free!*

God says when we truly receive His healing, that's exactly what we experience—*exhilarating, exuberant, infectious joy!*

Or if you don't like being compared to a cow, how about a majestic bird? David says in Psalm 103:1–5 that when you are forgiven and healed by God, "your youth is renewed like the eagle's." The freed heart—the virgin heart—is a youthful heart, soaring high on life's winds, excited about existence, viewing every day as an adventure. And I might point out that the youthfulness of one's heart in no way depends on whether one's hair is dark or gray.

Now, let me embellish on the calf analogy. By way of contrast, picture an old milk cow. She doesn't leap out of the stall; she saunters. *No hurry,* she cogitates. *Take your time. Everything's the same anyway. Same fields, same salt lick, same fences. Ho hum. Yesterday, today, tomorrow—they're all the same. That's my life.*

A heart in bondage is like a sauntering cow. It moves, loves, and lives without passion, energy, or joy. A sexually bonded heart can't leap forward because it expends all of its energy trying to redeem, justify, hide, and forget the past. That's enough to drain the leap out of anyone.

David describes his leap-less condition well in Psalm 38:4–10:

> My guilt has overwhelmed me
> like a burden too heavy to bear.

My wounds fester and are loathsome
because of my sinful folly.
I am bowed down and brought very low;
all day long I go about mourning.
My back is filled with searing pain;
there is no health in my body.
I am feeble and utterly crushed;
I groan in anguish of heart.
All my longings lie open before you, O LORD;
my sighing is not hidden from you.
My heart pounds, my strength fails me;
even the light has gone from my eyes.

What overwhelming guilt was David carrying? So heavy and debilitating that his back hurt, and he felt weak, bowed over, physically sick?

David had had sex with another man's wife. And then when she became pregnant, in order to hide his sin he had her husband killed. He was an adulterer and a murderer. That's a lot of guilt to bear.

I, too, was an adulterer and a murderer. Like David, I felt weighed down under a heavy burden. I was lonely, afraid, depressed, anxious.

I felt old. Yes old. *Old* and *tired* are words I remember using often to describe my inner condition. I sauntered from one long day to the next identically long day, heavy-hearted, living a partial life.

Not anymore.

When God healed me I suddenly felt young. My enthusiasm for life returned. I could relate to the calf and the eagle. Inside I was doing cartwheels and handsprings. I discovered the fountain of youth—the eternal divine gift of a leaping and soaring spirit.

God's healing power inspired David to do some leaping and soaring of his own:

> *You turned my wailing into dancing;*
> *you removed my sackcloth and clothed me with joy,*
> *that my heart may sing to you and not be silent.*
> *O LORD my God, I will give you thanks forever.*
> *(Psalm 30:11–12)*

A miracle! The guy with the aching back is now dancing. Instead of sighing, he's singing. In place of groaning and complaining, he's thanking God. He was a cow (well, a bull, I guess); now he's a calf. His head, once bowed down in shame, is soaring high like an eagle's. That's a miracle—one that impacted him, not only spiritually, but also emotionally and physically.

I recognize the symptoms. It happened to me.

Are you feeling old? A child of God, forgiven and healed, may *be* old on the outside, but never need *feel* old on the inside.

If you're feeling inwardly ancient, maybe you need to visit the Burden Bearer for an injection of youth. He'll take your heart back to the days when you were still a virgin.

Freedom From/Freedom To

Since God began to renew my virgin heart, I have created an ever-growing list of freedoms that come with it. Some are freedoms *from* burdens, pain, and loss. And some are freedoms *to* blessings and great gifts.

I experience freedom:

- from feeling bonded to my past sins and their consequences.
- from a feeling of darkness in my life.
- from shame.
- from the hold of certain sins over me.
- from the coping mechanisms I used for numbing the feelings of pain and shame.
- from self-absorption, thinking everything was about me.
- from self-protection, indecisiveness, defensiveness, control.
- from secrecy, never revealing the true me.
- from masks, outward appearances to protect myself from rejection.
- from stagnation in my relationships with others and God.
- from perfectionism, the exhausting need to be right, good, and acceptable all the time.
- from performance, the need to redeem my sins through service.
- from pride, the kind by which I masked my low sense of self-worth.

I have freedom:

- to feel again, to enjoy the roller coaster of emotions—sadness and joy, rather than numbness.
- to love freely, to give true love to my family instead of self-centered love.

- to be vulnerable, to risk giving myself emotionally in my relationships, without the need to protect.
- to be open and honest, no more guarded secrets.
- to serve because *God* has called me to service, not because I need self-redemption.
- to say no; now that I'm free of the need to perform, I no longer say yes out of obligation.
- to grow relationally; I can now become more intimate in my relationships with my husband and with God.
- to surrender, to give all of my heart to God, not just selected pieces.
- to be broken—brokenness no longer signifies weakness; it has become my strength.

An even more significant list is that of the destructive emotional and behavioral symptoms that my invisible bonds produced in me. When I started the postabortion Bible study, we filled out a symptom checklist indicating the strength of each symptom, using a zero-to-three scoring system, where three indicates extreme impact. (See the "Symptom Checklists" at the end of this book.)

As I read through the list for the first time, I became aware of current struggles that I had never acknowledged. Sometimes seeing something written out makes it "real." I had had concerns whenever these symptoms peeked through my veneer, but I usually stuffed them away and tried not to dwell on them. Now there they were in black and white, and I had to be truthful about how much they were hurting me.

I was shocked to discover that I scored most of the

items on this list with a two or three, meaning that I struggled significantly with them. Throughout the previous twenty-five years, I would have told you with absolute honesty that I was "just fine." I had become so skilled at coping that I was totally unaware of all the unhealthy and destructive outlets for my inner injuries.

Fast-forward to the end of the postabortion Bible study. My moment of truth came the day I completed the symptom checklist for the second time. Without referring to my first test—and having largely forgotten how I had first scored the symptoms—I honestly evaluated the extent to which each item now affected me.

When I put the two tests together I stared at them in disbelief. *They were all zeros and ones.* Not a two or three on the entire sheet. All the symptoms with which I experienced extreme struggles at the beginning of the study were now either minimized or eliminated.

I was amazed! On the outside I wept with joy. On the inside I was leaping and soaring.

I still am.

Miracles Waiting to Happen

Before that moment, I had a subjective awareness that I felt different. But God knew that I, being a scientist by nature, needed measurable proof. Now the evidence was staring me in the face. Once twos and threes, I was now zeros and ones. Nothing could have convinced me more conclusively. I knew now that God had done something in my life that was magnificent. Incredible. Beyond my wildest imagination.

I had just become a miracle.

Are you willing to trust God to make you a miracle? Or are you content just witnessing miracles? Are you happy living on half steam, or do you sometimes yearn to experience full-power living? Do you want to remain a sauntering cow, or become a leaping calf?

God says that His own fullness—His character, power, and promises—are in His Son, Jesus Christ (see Colossians 2:9). When we accept Christ as our Savior, God says that His fullness enters us through His Son. From that point on, we have all of God living in us, all the time. We have power, victory, and goodness at our disposal 24/7.

Looking back, I now see that bondage to my past had kept me from "attaining to the whole measure of the fullness of Christ" (Ephesians 4:13). The complete power source was fully available to me, but I was only drawing upon a small fraction of it.

My experience of healing has led me into full-power living. It has allowed me to forgive myself. To *feel* truly forgiven. To attain to the whole measure of the fullness of Christ. My heart was once a heart of stone, but now it's a heart of flesh (Ezekiel 36:26). My head was once bowed low, but now it's held high (Leviticus 26:13). I used to saunter like an old cow, but now I leap like a baby calf (Malachi 4:2). Instead of shame, God has heaped on me a double portion of His grace, mercy, and joy (Isaiah 61:7). Pride was once my "strength," but now I delight in brokenness.

I am a miracle.

God has given me a virgin heart.

ABANDONED HEART

Opening Your Heart to God and Others

Abandoned, adj., 1. wholly free from restraint

Abandoned heart, n., 1. a heart that is wholly free from restraint and therefore able to take risks

God grant me the senility to forget the people I don't like,
the opportunity to run into the people I do like,
and the ability to remember the difference.

THE SENILITY PRAYER

recently read, on a coffee mug, this playful poke at the "Serenity Prayer" (which I appreciate and respect, by the way). I share it with you now because it highlights the center around which all else in life revolves—*relationships*.

Everything that truly matters is relational. Our greatest joys and deepest struggles involve relationships. We were all born with the same universal need and desire to initiate and maintain healthy relationships. This is the essence of who we are and who we were created to be. Many things in life bring happiness: money, fame, sensual pleasure, recognition, luxury, toys. But none of these have any meaning without someone to share them with. In fact, some are impossible apart from interaction between people.

Celebrities Clint Eastwood and Tom Hanks were asked to describe their level of happiness with all their wealth and fame. Their answer was enlightening for the vast majority of us who will experience neither in this life. They said their greatest joy and meaning came from their relationships—their families and friends.[1]

We are relational because God is relational. He created us because He longed for relationships with us. Into the depths of our souls He put an insatiable desire that only He can satisfy. Once He fills that niche, then joy infuses our experience of everything else—every relationship, every possession, and every achievement.

When we think ahead to the end of life, all of us know at some level that it won't be money or fame that will comfort us, but the people who have become most important to us. Yet we easily forget this. A very good friend of mine who achieved financial success provides us with the right perspective: "I measure my wealth by the company I keep."

The Price Tag on Relationships

If relationships are the most important commodity in the world, then why don't we throw ourselves into them with *unrestrained abandon*? If God and people are the investment that will provide greatest satisfaction for our hearts, why do we spend so much time and effort striving instead for every-thing else—pursuits that fuel our discontent, leaving us always wanting more?

Perhaps it's because relationships come at a price. Not dollars and cents, but lavish investments of time and effort. And in many cases, we conclude that *the price is too high.*

It's easier to write a check to World Vision than to take off a week to go in person and help the needy. It's easier to send an e-mail than to make a call. It's easier to tell people that I'm praying for them than to stop and pray with them.

And then there's the greatest price of all. *Risk of pain.* I'd rather do almost anything than risk being rejected, hurt, and manipulated by someone else, even if I love him or her. That's the barrier that stops many of us short of abandon in relation-ships. Relationships—true, intimate, vulnerable relationships—require that we risk incurring the very wounds and losses we spend our lives trying to avoid.

Sometimes the price seems way too high for us to pay.

Guess what. It *is* too high for *us* to pay.

That's why you can't break through to an abandoned heart without God's help. By yourself, you'll probably never break free from the fears that come from sexual wounding—especially when the outcome is unpredictable. Until God is the one who fills your God-sized void, you probably won't even try.

An abandoned heart, which is willing to risk true inti-macy, requires *brokenness.*

Now, don't be alarmed. Brokenness doesn't mean you'll become a martyr, a doormat, or an emotional victim in your relationships. The way I'm using the word, brokenness is simply the opposite of pride.

The first line in Rick Warren's bestselling book, *The Purpose Driven Life*,[2] is: "It's not about you." What a compelling statement! In our human nature, we are constantly driven to make everything about us. But God says that the purpose and fulfillment of life comes when we make everything about Him. And when we place Him at the center, we also choose to make life about selfless, interdependent relationships with other people.

We cannot have open, intimate relationships—with God or with anyone else—without brokenness. There is no other way.

I know that now. I wish I'd known it sooner. I wish I had submitted to brokenness long ago, before I wasted decades pursuing all the counterfeits.

Brokenness and pride. Two opposite motives battling against each other in our hearts. How can you tell which holds sway inside you?

In answer, let me share with you a portion of Nancy Leigh DeMoss's[3] list of contrasts between the characteristics of proud people and broken people. As you read the two lists ask God to reveal the condition of your heart.

Proud People...	Broken People...
Have independent, self-sufficient spirits	Have dependent spirits, recognizing their need for others
Are selfishly protective of their time, their rights, and their reputation	Are biblically self-denying
Desire to be served	Are motivated to serve others
Feel confident in how much they know	Are humbled by how very much they have to learn

Proud People...	Broken People...
Keep others at arms length	Are willing to risk getting close to others and to take risks of loving intimately
Are unapproachable or defensive when criticized	Receive criticism with a humble, open spirit
Have a hard time saying, "I was wrong; will you please forgive me?"	Are quick to admit failure and to seek forgiveness when necessary
Are concerned about the consequences of their sin	Are grieved over the cause, the root of their sin

What drives your heart—the characteristics of pride or the qualities of brokenness? Is everything all about you? Or has brokenness and healing freed you to make it about God and others?

The Strength of a Broken Heart

Humbling exercise, isn't it? When I first read that list of contrasts, I was amazed that my friends and family could tolerate me at all. When I realized that my thoughts, attitudes, words, and actions in all my relationships were fueled by selfish pride, I experienced my greatest moment of humility. At age forty-five, I still wanted everything to be about me.

As part of the healing process, God began to move more of me from the proud side over to the broken side. And He's not finished with me. When I'm tempted to trust myself rather than God, I'm still very capable of speaking and acting from the proud side. I rely on the daily discipline of asking God to break me, and He often answers by showing me where I need to realign.

Why does an abandoned heart require brokenness? Because a heart abandoned to vulnerable intimacy must be strong. Not strong in self-centered protectiveness, but strong in the selfless qualities of brokenness.

Brokenness empowers us to risk a new way of loving, a new way of living, a new way of relating. Abandonment to intimacy can't happen in the context of the old patterns of thought and emotion—fear and protectiveness. So brokenness changes us, giving us a new "operating system"—new thoughts, new attitudes, new actions.

If you've experienced healing and forgiveness, then you are acquainted with brokenness. And once broken, your attitude changes to become "the same as that of Christ Jesus: Who, being in very nature God, did not consider equality with God something to be grasped, but made himself nothing, taking the very nature of a servant, being made in human likeness...he humbled himself and became obedient to death—even death on a cross!" (Philippians 2:5–8).

When it comes to brokenness, Jesus Christ leads the way. He's God, and yet He humbled Himself *for us*. The Creator submitted to His creation; the Holy One became the sacrifice for the unholy. Jesus wanted us so much that He was willing to die to have us. That's ultimate brokenness. Deepest love.

Maximum risk.

Jesus left the decision to accept Him and His sacrificial gift in our hands. Our wanting Him in return is left to us as a matter of individual will. Jesus risked rejection, abuse, and hate from us, and yet He sacrificed everything anyway.

I can't imagine how.

His brokenness defeated the hold of the enemy and

unleashed the power of God. In brokenness, He desired us more than He feared the risk.

And our brokenness will do the same. It gives us moral strength. It defeats the hold of sin in our lives. It breaks our old patterns of relating, and it unleashes the power of God, so that we are supernaturally able to love unconditionally and to risk intimacy with an abandoned heart.

Broken Hearts and Cracked Pipes

I once heard insanity defined as "doing the same thing over and over again, expecting a different result." This definition works well for describing the way we avoid brokenness and true intimacy when building lifelong relationships.

We humans are experts at substituting a variety of strategies in our attempts to achieve true intimacy—any strategy but brokenness. None of the substitutes work. And the more they don't work, the more desperately we revisit them. Over and over. Insanely.

In chapter 4, we examined the dynamic of couples who achieve a short-lived *feeling* of intimacy through an early sexual debut. But, you may recall, this is like opening the valve on a cracked steam pipe; it relieves the pressure so that the couple can ignore the cracks—the needs in the relationship that can only be met by the hard, consistent work of nonsexual communication.

When the short-term Novocain of sex wears off, showing that it doesn't work, insanity presides, and more sex becomes the "solution" for the dysfunctional relationship.

The sexual bond makes the couple feel closer than they actually are, and this leads to premature marriage commitments between couples who don't really know each other. I believe this bond and the blindness it causes are the reasons that so many marriages end in divorce. They end, that is, after reality rudely removes the blinders some years, months, or days into the marriage.

A couple who wants true intimacy and a lifelong commitment must do the work required for growing in intimacy. Hard work. Work that can only be done by broken people.

It's the work of facing and communicating through conflict.

Gary Smalley, in his book *Secrets to Lasting Love,*[4] says,

> If you're going to dive to the deepest levels [of intimacy], conflict is not only the wall, it's also the door. Yes, conflict, handled constructively, is the power that can propel your relationship through the doorway that separates superficial relationships from profound ones.... The problem is, most couples don't see conflict as the doorway to a better, more satisfying relationship. They see the wall of conflict as a place of either victory or defeat, not a means for learning life's most valuable lessons. And so they fall before the wall, caught up in the force that is the universal destroyer of relationships: mishandled conflict.

Only broken people have the strength and courage for this challenge.

Proud people are weak people. They give in easily to the insanity of sex-as-intimacy. Roger Hillerstrom writes, "Sex can even be used to avoid intimacy.... Sexually active couples often use the sensation of [sexual] intimacy to deny the existence of conflict. A couple can go to bed, feel great about each other, and never resolve the real issue. Problems don't get resolved, they just get buried under artificial intimacy."[5]

For a while, maybe years, this will work. At first, you may not realize how lonely you feel within your marriage. But eventually the deep longing of your heart will drive you to seek that intimacy in other places or with other people. I'm not suggesting that close, intimate relationships outside marriage are always a bad thing. But whenever we replace what we should be experiencing with our spouse with something or someone else, we rob each other of what God intended for our marriage. Whether it's work, hobbies, possessions, friends, children, or an emotional or sexual affair, we will seek through some surrogate the intimacy we're missing with our spouse.

I described in chapter 4 the intimacy deficit I sensed between my husband and me. But for decades I left it alone. It was too risky to venture into. Much safer to talk about the kids, work, or plans for the weekend. I can't count the number of times I lay next to my "best friend," silently yearning to share the depths of my heart. Words formed in my head, but I could not will them to come out of my mouth.

I was not yet broken. I could not give myself to my husband—or to anyone else—with abandon.

While reviewing my journal recently, I came across this entry, dated March 29, 2004:

Saturday night as Eric and I were talking, I realized that for some reason I couldn't share myself deeply with him. I can't get it out of my mind that maybe if we hadn't had sex early in our relationship I would have recognized that this was not someone I could be a soul mate with. I want someone I can talk to for hours and hours.

That's when we followed Hillerstrom's advice and abstained from sex for a month. For the first time we closed the pressure valve and paid attention to the steam pipe cracks that needed repair and maintenance.

We talked.

We became broken.

We grew in strength and courage.

We gave way to abandon and risk.

We experienced level-five intimacy for the first time ever.

Recently Eric and I completed an intimacy checkup. How strong is our emotional connection? Are we making progress?

I'm happy to report that our relationship has grown significantly. Our commitment is stronger, and our intimacy is deeper. Testimony to God's grace in our lives.

I now know that as the hair gets grayer and as the kids leave the nest, I'm going to love growing old with this man by my side. He's my best friend.

Abandoning Finger-Pointing

Do you feel hopelessly stuck in a relationship or marriage that began with an intimacy handicap? Do you feel robbed of the deep companionship for which your heart longs, but which you now realize you'll never have?

Don't despair. God is teaching Eric and me that regardless of the way our marriage began, He can transform it into all it was meant to become. And He desires to do the same for you. You can begin today to create the intimate bond of which you unintentionally cheated yourselves.

I read a great quote from John Maxwell's book *Today Matters*.[6] He uses the quote to encourage the pursuit of health and exercise, but I thought it applied perfectly to our pursuit of intimate relationships: "Though you cannot go back and make a brand-new start, my friend, you can start now and make a brand-new end." You may have started this relationship all wrong, but you can begin today to make sure it ends right.

It starts with you. When it comes to relationships, the only way God will change the other person is if you are willing to let Him change you first.

I know, that's scary. We've come full circle to humility and brokenness again. Annoying, isn't it? Every time I go to God with complaints about my spouse, God brings out the list of things I need to work on. The first thing He showed me was that the lack of emotional intimacy in our relationship was *my* fault, not my husband's. That was a shocking revelation. All this time I had smugly assumed that it was his fault; he was the boring one. But God showed me that I was the one holding back; it was *my* fault that we lacked the depth of intimacy I desired.

God showed me that this was pride—the opposite of brokenness, the bane of abandonment and intimacy. It was all about me and my desperate aversion to pain, rejection, or manipulation. Even in my marriage, I unconsciously protected myself. I consistently withdrew from him physically and emotionally. It wasn't just sex that I drew back from, but simple hugs and kisses as well. Emotionally, when prompted to share things with him, I would say nothing. I was short on praise but articulate with criticism. I was angry, unforgiving, and judgmental. I would overreact to the smallest irritations, and my "love" was conditional and controlling.

148

A HEART SET FREE

Yikes! *I* don't even like that me.

And yet this incredible man not only hung in there, but extended unconditional love in return.

I'm so grateful to him for living with me so patiently, until I discovered the brokenness and abandonment that allowed our intimacy to grow at last.

The Beginning of Brokenness

How can you find an abandoned heart? How can you live and love in brokenness…in true intimacy? How can you be the kind of person with whom someone would want a life-long relationship?

Well…*you* can't.

But God can. Through you. The beginning of the journey—for everyone—toward this kind of heart, and the life fulfillment it brings, is a relationship with God.

How is *your* relationship with God? Recently in a Bible study I took Hillerstrom's five levels of human intimacy, and I applied them to the process of growth in relationship with God. Here is the new list I came up with:[7]

Lowest Level: Knowledge *about* God

Low Level: Learning about God from others

Moderate Level: Begin a relationship with God; begin to know God—limited sharing with Him

High Level: Sharing more of ourselves with God—feelings, desires, struggles

Highest Level: Completely surrendered to God; able to have complete openness and honesty with Him about everything—our shameful past, our doubts, our fears, our hopes…everything

God already knows each of us at the highest level of intimacy. He knows us better than we know ourselves. Psalm 139 says that He discerns all our ways and knows our very words before we speak them (vv. 3–4). That is true intimacy. Even if you haven't given God a moment's thought your whole life, He already knows you completely.

Does that alarm you? It needn't. The amazing story of the gospel is that even when God knew every last shameful secret, and before we had the slightest thought of Him, He wanted to have a relationship with us at the highest level of intimacy.

I often ask God, "With all You know about me, why do You want a relationship with me?" I won't completely understand until I see Him face-to-face. But for now I believe Him when He says that before He created me He already loved me. It has nothing to do with who I am, how I think, or what I've done. It's because of who *He* is. He loves me because He chooses to, not because I've earned it.

So God already relates to you at the highest level. What about the other lane of this two-way street? At what level do *you* relate to *Him?* Do you know about Him at the lowest level, without yet being willing to pursue knowing Him personally? Or have you moved up a level, a little closer to knowing Him by seeking answers from others who already know Him?

Maybe you've progressed bravely and humbly to the moderate level—you've taken the first step in a relationship with Him. If you've asked Jesus to forgive your sins and come in and take control of your life, then you have stepped onto the path that leads to everything we've talked about in this book—complete forgiveness and healing.

If you've never asked Christ into your life and given Him complete control, I invite you to pray the following prayer (or something along these lines; your attitude is more important than the words):

> Dear Jesus,
>
> I acknowledge that You are God. I believe that You died on the cross for my sins and that, by accepting Your gift of salvation, I am forgiven for all my past, present, and future sins. I invite You into my heart. I ask You to take control of my life. I thank You for the gift of eternal life, which means that when I die I will live with You forever. Thank You for Your incredible gift. Amen.

If you've just expressed this heart desire to God, then welcome to the family of God! You'll find that we're not perfect, but we're a big, loving brood of brothers and sisters. We'll welcome you with open arms.

If you've just joined the family today, or very recently, I encourage you to pray and ask God to lead you to a church that teaches His Word, loves Him, and reaches the world for Christ. If you log on to www.billygraham.org, you will discover some excellent resources to facilitate your new growth. Follow the link "Finding Jesus" on the home page. There you will find an invitation to receive materials to help guide you in your Christian walk.

If you've moved beyond the moderate level, then you

have truly begun to know God. You are becoming deeply intimate with the God of the universe. The degree of depth and intimacy you enjoy with God will grow in direct proportion to the degree of humility and brokenness you're willing to accept. He says that when we humble ourselves before Him, He will lift us up (see James 4:10). Ironic, isn't it? The lower we bow, the greater our elevation...closer to Him.

No matter where you are on the intimacy scale, ask yourself what's keeping you from moving to the next level. If you're not sure, ask God; He knows. Maybe you're ignoring something that God is asking you to do. Or *not* to do.

"Humility" without obedience is a myth. If you don't obey, you can't move on. If you've been stalled at a certain level with God for a long time, check with Him to see what's causing the holdup. Then do something about it right away. Regardless of the seeming difficulty of His request, I'm confident you'll be pleased with the results.

God's Work...and Ours

In chapter 6, I took you through five steps for breaking invisible sexual bonds from the past. The fifth step in particular—praying to break the bonds—involved inviting God to work a series of miracles in our lives, severing one by one the unseen ties that we've created.

Now let me explain several ways you can actively cooperate with God's healing work inside you—steps you can take in order to facilitate true intimacy in your relationships, especially your marriage.

When you read about some of these steps, you'll think, *No problem.* To others, you'll respond, *No way!* But don't trust your first reaction. Ask God to soften your heart to make you willing to do whatever it takes.

In fact, the first step you must take is a decision to commit wholeheartedly to growing in your relationship, no matter how difficult it gets. I guarantee, the moment you move in this direction, something will tempt you to quit. *This is hopeless. It will never change.* These were the defeating thoughts that often invaded my mind. Don't give in to the enemy's attempt to thwart your mission. He will try, but your resolve will cause him to flee (see James 4:7).

Let's start with one of the hard ones. If you're not married and you're having sex, stop immediately. It doesn't matter how long you've been together or how close you are, or even if you're planning to get married. You need to stop now. If you're living together, one of you needs to move out. Sex is clouding your judgment, stagnating your intimacy, and stunting your spiritual, emotional, and relational growth.

These might be the most difficult words in this book for you to hear. But I promise that if you break through to obedience, God will provide you with courage to follow it through to great reward.

On the other hand, if you're married and you've retained any emotional or physical ties with past lovers, cut them off. Now. End all calls, e-mails, and meetings. You cannot continue a friendship with a past lover and, at the same time, grow more intimate with your spouse.

One newly married man confided in "Dear Abby" that his wife's friendship with past lovers was troubling him and causing a problem in his marriage. He said that continuing the friendship "opens a window of opportunity for the guy to make advances when she's at a low point."[8] That's an excellent comment. You don't *feel* love for your spouse every day, and on one of those low days, when you're experiencing difficulties in your marriage, you will be tempted to confide in the past lover rather than in your spouse. It only takes one small wedge to create a vast divide.

Remove any evidence of past lovers from your life. I know this may sound trivial, but consider another young man, terribly hurt by his wife's constant reminders of her past: "Although I know Jane loves me and her exes mean nothing to her now, she still mentions their names in passing every so often. She still has photos of them, old letters, and gifts. It's a constant reminder of her past."[9] As long as Jane stays tied to her past, this relationship will never move forward.

How about you? Still have old photos lying around, maybe a special love letter or gift? It's time to get rid of them. Their presence may seem harmless, but they're creating a subconscious wall between you and the one with whom you want a life commitment. You may simply have to trust me on this; you might not see the danger of the reminders or the benefit of their removal until after the tie is broken.

Even if you've broken off communication and removed physical evidence of past lovers, they're still in your *mind.* That's harder to deal with, but not impossible. Praying the prayer to break sexual bonds will not erase their memory, but will break the strength of their hold on you. When you pray this way, you unleash the power of God; now your memory no longer controls you, but you control it.

God has given us a secret weapon that we can access anywhere, anytime. It allows us to control our minds. Second Corinthians 10:4–5 describes the only weapon that can continue to provide us victory over our haunting memories: "The weapons we fight with are not the weapons of the world. On the contrary, they have divine power to demolish strong-holds. We demolish arguments and every pretension that sets itself up against the knowledge of God, and *we take captive every thought* to make it obedient to Christ" (emphasis mine).

How do you take a thought captive? It's simple, but takes some practice. The more you do it, the more efficient and successful you'll be. Here's how I do it.

Imagine that your mind is a room with a door. In order for a thought to enter your mind, it must first knock. The door has a little window, so you can preview the thought before it enters. The instant you decide to shut the window to keep the thought out—rather than opening the door and letting it in—is the moment you take the thought captive. Why captive? Because Christ is on the other side of that door waiting to overpower it the moment you surrender it to him—the instant you shut your window.

Impure thoughts, fantasies, emotional affairs, porno-graphic images. Or debilitating emotions like fear, despair, or resentment. Taking them captive gives you immediate con-trol. As soon as I recognize a thought that I don't want to enter my mind, I immediately pray, *Lord, I take this thought captive and surrender it to You. Please remove this thought and replace it with Your truth.*

It's a powerful weapon! Why? Because behind it is God's power at work.

The more you practice this, the better you'll get, and the less often and less forcefully those thoughts will come knocking.

Every time I allow a thought in, my appetite for it grows. The more I deny access, the less I desire it. I can never stop with just one bite of chocolate. The only way to resist is not to take the first taste. After a while, I don't crave it anymore, and when the temptation arises, I've lost interest.

Starve the thought and it will die.

By removing the emotional, physical, and mental ties to the past, you remove the restraints from your heart, allowing yourself to move forward with abandon in your most important relationships. Then you are ready to do whatever is necessary for true intimacy. The work isn't over, but the hardest part is done, and you're well on your way to the relationships you've longed to have with God and with your current or future spouse.

"Cope" or Go "Broke"

I've discovered that a broken, abandoned heart releases me from being defensive and allows me to surrender to God and my husband with greater trust. Along with this brokenness comes freedom from all the counterfeits I've tried to use in its place.

What is your favorite counterfeit? Is it shopping, excessive time with friends, flirting, your children, an emotional or sexual affair? Are you a superservant in your community, church, or children's school, numbing your heart with busyness? How about excessive use of e-mail, Internet, or countless games of solitaire? Maybe to avoid emotional and physical intimacy you watch TV or absorb yourself in a book until you hear those safe, familiar sounds of snoring coming from the bedroom. Maybe it's drugs or alcohol. Do you need a glass of wine to become vulnerable physically and emotionally? Do you use it to deaden your feelings?

These are called coping mechanisms, survival tactics, safety nets. You used to need them because you knew no other way. *But not anymore.* An abandoned heart doesn't desire or need a counterfeit. No matter what your past coping methods, God will lovingly challenge you to trust Him instead. One by one, He will ask you to release each imposter and commit your faith to the real thing—Himself.

Start by asking Him to reveal which coping mechanisms you're using. Our initial reaction is to cling to them with desperation, because they have become part of our identity, and we cherish the temporary security we've received from them in the past. *Let them go.* Start with the one God is bringing to mind right now. God will replace it with Himself. If you'll give Him a chance—if you'll fall into His hands with abandon—you will forget you ever needed anything else.

Beyond This Book

Many marriages have serious problems that require marriage counseling, in addition to the healing measures I've shared with you. For example, if your relationship has been damaged by infidelity, pornography, or sexual perversion, then professional Christian counseling is a necessary part of your healing and recovery. You might need to separate from your spouse for a time as you work through some of these tough issues. (Please do this while under the care of a trained professional.)

If you or your children are in danger of physical or sexual abuse, please do whatever is necessary to ensure safety. Don't fool yourself into believing you can achieve true intimacy with someone who is harming you. A safe environment is a critical requirement. If you're not sure what to do, ask God, ask a godly person, or make an appointment with a Christian counselor. God uses the lips of others who love and follow

Him to confirm what He's telling you in your heart.

In any of these circumstances, *pray.* Surrender to God every step in your journey toward abandonment, and ask Him to intervene in your relationships, especially your marriage. He eagerly longs to transform your mistakes into something incredibly beautiful.

The God who has the power to break your past sexual bonds also has the power to create a new bond between you and your spouse.

Did you catch that? No matter what the chemistry of your marriage—and I mean "chemistry" literally (see chapter 3)—or how your relationship began, He can create a brand-new bond between you. In Matthew 19:26, Jesus said, "With man this is impossible, but with God all things are possible." Absolutely nothing is impossible with Him. The scientific community may not believe that, but remember: They only study science; God *created* it. After my experiences with God, I know He's not only capable of something this remarkable, He's *remarkably* capable.

Has this chapter overwhelmed you? It seems like a lot, doesn't it? God didn't reveal all of this to me at the same time, thank goodness. He knows I wouldn't even have taken the first step.

Don't concern yourself with the whole journey. Just start with the one thing God is asking you to do *today.* Your step today will lead, under His guidance, to the next step of your journey tomorrow, and then the next day. And then through the days, weeks, and months that follow. Soon you'll look back and marvel over your progress, how much you've changed, and the path God used to get you here.

The changes you make not only impact you, but also

your spouse, your children, your friends, your church, and your community.

Sound inconceivable? Remember, it's not about you. Every choice you make affects everyone around you, positively or negatively. Your decision to live with an abandoned heart will serve as an inspiration to those around you as they pursue true intimacy with God and others.

It may not be *about* you, but it does *begin* with your decision. With the decision to accept a broken and abandoned heart.

Brokenness and pride. Two powerful, opposing forces that shape relationships.

Which one drives you?

WISE HEART

Dating Wisdom for Singles

wise, adj., 1. marked by deep understanding, keen discernment, and a capacity for sound judgment

wise heart, n., 1. a heart that operates with understanding, discernment, and sound judgment

But the wisdom that comes from heaven is first of all pure;
then peace-loving, considerate, submissive,
full of mercy and good fruit, impartial and sincere.

JAMES 3:17

D id you know there are two kinds of wisdom? This was new to me. I assumed there was one form of wisdom, and you either possessed it or didn't. But the Bible says there are indeed two: worldly wisdom and heavenly wisdom.

According to James, worldly wisdom is fueled by bitter

envy and selfish ambition (v. 14). In other words, by pride. Heavenly wisdom, on the other hand, is fueled by just the opposite: humility and brokenness.

Recently I received this imploring e-mail from a friend: "I'm needing courage to pray and ask God to show me where my pride is and to break me of it. Yikes, I don't even like saying that. Almost everything spiritual I put my hands on lately talks about humility! Okay, I get the message. Any wise words?"

Can you relate to her? I responded by saying that pride makes us weak, but humility makes us strong. How? By making us wise.

Earlier in his letter, James says, "Who is wise and understanding among you? Let him show it by his good life, by deeds done in the humility that comes from wisdom" (v. 13). So being wise makes you humble.

But the connection goes the other way, too. Being humble also makes you wise. Solomon, the wisest man ever to live, wrote in Proverbs 9:10, "The fear of the LORD is the beginning of wisdom." To fear the Lord means to exhibit a loving reverence for God that includes submission to His lordship and to the commands of His words. When you fear God, you are humbling yourself before Him. You're acknowledging Him as Master of your life. For us, this is the greatest act of humility.

The result? From this humble wisdom, James concludes, comes a life that is "pure; then peace-loving, considerate, submissive, full of mercy and good fruit, impartial and sincere" (James 3:17).

It seems backward, doesn't it? How can we exude wisdom if we acknowledge that we're not wise, that we don't know everything? Aren't you tempted, as I am, to do just the opposite—to boast about your accomplishments and knowledge to prove your wisdom? To gain respect? To feel loved?

But what kind of fruit does this strategy bear? My boasting distances me from people, reveals my insecurities, and strains my closest relationships. Where's the wisdom in that?

In contrast, as God broke and humbled me, I discovered an unexpected benefit. People were drawn to me because of my humility. They trusted me. They saw God working in my life and wanted to learn from me. As I reflect in amazement on all of this, I am humbled even more.

I guess we shouldn't be so surprised. It *was* God who chose to come to earth, not as a King, high and mighty on a royal throne, but as a humble baby. His throne a bed of hay, His palace an animal stall. Now that's humility. We will never out-humble God. He has the wisest heart of all.

Wisdom at Work

What kind of wisdom have you been using: worldly wisdom or godly wisdom? Not sure? Look at the fruit of your life for the answer. Worldly wisdom leads to "disorder and every evil practice," James says (v. 16). Have your choices led to chaos and disorder? Have some of your actions been impure, inconsiderate, or contrary to peace? Do you look back on your decisions with satisfaction or with shame?

Don't despair. Even if you've lived unwisely up to this point, God always makes abundant wisdom freely available. You just have to ask.

James 1:5 says, "If any of you lacks wisdom, he should ask God, who gives *generously* to all without finding fault, and it will be given to him" (emphasis mine).

Is wisdom your desire? Do you want to make God-wise choices about your relationships? When you're ready to give up doing things your way and surrender to God's way, wisdom will begin to flow. It won't happen overnight or without some humbling in the process. But one day when you least expect it, you'll realize you're making wise choices. You'll be producing peace, not chaos. Joy instead of regret. Purity in place of shame.

Let me share the story of a woman who followed her own worldly wisdom. It wasn't all her fault. She inherited her wisdom from her father. At the center of his worldview was the assumption that a woman's only true value is in what she can offer a man sexually. Unfortunately, her father clearly implied this worldly lie before she even knew what sex was.

How did this wisdom guide her life? Straight into sexual relationships with men, under the illusion that she was earning love. Young men, older men, the *wrong* men. When I met her, her third husband had just left, abandoning her with three children from different fathers and a confused, broken, wounded heart. Driven by her need for a new bonding experience, Melissa had already moved in with another man, and was on her way to making him husband number four.

Until God intervened. Recognizing the futility of her actions, and feeling the despair of yet another unfulfilling relationship, she responded to God's leading to come back to church. And there she learned a new way. She had already begun to operate in God's wisdom when I met with her that morning to hear her story. She wanted to join my Bible study on sexual healing, and I knew she was ready. With only God's guidance she had already moved herself and her daughter out of her latest partner's home and into their own apartment.

For the first time she knew in her heart that sex before marriage was wrong. She wanted to follow God's way.

I was proud of her. As I watched her struggle through the pain of her growth over the next few weeks, her resolve to follow God never faltered. Her humility before God led her to make wise choices for her future—physically, emotionally, and spiritually. But her wise choices impacted others as well. Several months after the study ended, Melissa wanted to meet with me. I didn't recognize her. I was looking at a new woman. I saw life and strength in her face, heard it in her voice, and felt it in her embrace. Obviously, God hadn't stopped working when the study finished. In fact, He had only begun.

Melissa shared an amazing story with me. Her daughter, caught in the same lies, had been living with her boyfriend. Although their relationship was strained, Melissa began to share what God was teaching her in our study and the changes she was making because of it. Her daughter's heart began to soften, and as a result realized that she wanted what her mother had. She moved out of her boyfriend's place, stopped having sex with him, and began attending church. No wonder Melissa was so excited. What is more, the boyfriend had agreed to this new arrangement and was attending church as well.

God has given Melissa a new wisdom to guide her children's lives. With it she has broken the cycle of sinful lies that she previously allowed to direct her path and her children's path. If God had not intervened, the same worldly wisdom would have perpetuated down into her grandchildren's lives.

Godly wisdom in our lives spreads ripples of unlimited impact that affect everyone around us, now and for generations to come.

It's contagious. It glorifies God. And it's eternal.

Melissa's story is a perfect example of the contrast between godly wisdom and worldly wisdom. What she's reaping now is the result of her humble choice to follow God. Her own worldly wisdom led to family crisis and personal chaos. God's wisdom is fulfilling her heart's desires in unexpected ways that are exceeding her wildest imagination.

Does your heart need new wisdom? Are you tired of doing relationships your way and failing? Are you ready for new direction? New focus?

New results?

If you've been following the steps in this book so far, then I trust God has led you to a place of humble dependence on Him. If this is the case, you're ready to ask the million-dollar question. It's a question everyone needs to ask, but it's especially pertinent to a single person seeking to find and cultivate a lifelong commitment to a marriage partner.

Here's the question: What is the *wisest* way to build intimacy? Not what *seems* right or best to you, but what's the God-wise way to build a relationship with impact that will outlast this life?

Give Yourself a Break

If you're divorced, have never been married, or are in a romantic relationship right now, then true intimacy is one of your most pressing concerns. You will only find it through wisdom.

In this chapter, I'll be speaking especially to those who have created sexual bonds in your past, who are determined that your next sexual bond will be the right one, the last one. The *lasting* one. That's my goal for you, too.

Whole books are devoted to Christian dating. In just this one chapter, I'll only be able to provide a brief overview. I suggest that you read some great books on the topic, especially the ones I've quoted throughout this book.

Meanwhile, let me share with you briefly what God has taught me in this area through my own experiences and research, and through counseling and teaching others.

If you've just come out of a relationship or a succession of them, then the first thing you need is time. Time to heal, time to reflect, time to discover yourself and God.

Dr. Donald Joy, in *Re-bonding: Preventing and Restoring Damaged Relationships,*[1] says that people who have created sexual bonds need time to heal and recharge before they move into the next relationship. He suggests that these people have "to go through a kind of 'detox' period, so they can recharge their sexual magnet if they are going to get healed. Yet most of these folks go right from one bed to another."

In chapter 3 we saw that with each successive sexual relationship, you release less oxytocin. But when you stop creating new bonds, you prevent further decline in your capacity to produce your bonding hormone. Does God restore levels of oxytocin? I can't say for certain from a medical perspective. From a spiritual perspective I believe He can and does. But unless you allow Him sufficient time to break and heal your past bonds, you won't give God the opportunity.

So the only way to buy time to heal is through celibacy. *Stop having sex.* God is very clear on this topic. Sex is for marriage. While you're having sex outside marriage, you can't experience healing from past sexual injuries; you'll only create new ones.

Remember the steam pipe example? Closing the valve exposes the cracks. You can't fix problems that you can't see.

Rick Stedman wrote *Your Single Treasure*,[2] one of the most insightful books on single sexuality I've ever read. In it he recounts the story of an engaged couple who asked him to marry them. He declined, unless they agreed to remain celibate until the wedding. The woman was willing, but the man resisted. In the end, he reluctantly agreed to abstain.

Within a short time, without sex clouding his judgment and creating a smokescreen around their relationship, the man realized that his fiancé was emotionally unstable and manipulative. He was amazed to learn that she had used sex to control him. Only by removing it was he able to see that she had used it to trick and capture him.

Once they closed the valve and exposed the cracks in the relationship, they realized how little they knew of each other. They discovered that their personalities were unsuited to each other, and they wisely broke off the engagement.

Yes, the breakup was devastating. But their trauma was much less than if they had gone their separate ways *after* the wedding cake. Or worse, after the diapers.

When you change the quality of your relationship by abstinence, you'll be able to see how much your loved one values you. Other-centered love means being willing to give up my needs and rights when it's better for you. Giving up sex is in both of your best interest. If your partner is opposed to abstaining, consider what that says about the value he or she places on you and your relationship. If they're not willing to give up sex for you now, how much sacrificial love do think you can expect after you're married?

Be the One

According to Dr. Joy, the second thing you need is people.[3] He suggests that, in order for healing to take place, significant nonromantic relationships are a must.

Look for safe people who want to know you and whom you can know through honest, open communication. Maybe you're not sure what a healthy, intimate, nonromantic relationship looks like. Mia confessed that after several marriages and scores of unhealthy relationships, she certainly didn't know what to look for. As a woman now in her thirties, she had to throw out everything she thought she knew about building meaningful relationships. She was ready to start over. But she had a problem. She didn't know where to begin. She'd never learned how to have genuine friendships with men; all of her male relationships had included sex.

Before a friendship can exist, you have to find someone with whom you can *be* friends. But is anyone willing to be just friends these days?

I sat and read *Choosing God's Best: Wisdom for Lifelong Romance* by Dr. Don Raunikar one afternoon. Within twenty-four hours, I recommended it to ten single friends. I've read many books on dating, but this one resonated with me like none other. In it Dr. Raunikar describes an exchange with Jenny, one of his single clients.

"It sounds good," Jenny said, "but I don't understand how we are supposed to find this person—the one God has for us."[4]

Dr. Raunikar explained that Jenny "was certain there was something she should be doing to maximize her opportunities—places she should go, things she should do, people she should see."

I loved his response: "You don't have to *do* anything but concentrate on *being* the right person—the person God wants you to be—instead of *finding* the right person. Godly marriages are made by first living godly lives. It's God's responsibility to reveal whether you will marry and whom you will marry. The arrangement is up to Him."

Focusing on God, rather than on finding someone to marry, causes you to become the kind of person others with the same values would want to marry. Dr. Raunikar says, "By focusing on our relationship with God (the highest point), we will find ourselves not only filled with God but also drawn to others who are filled with God. The irony here is that we actually become more appealing to the very type of person we desire to marry."[5]

What a novel concept! Letting God have control. Often the wisest way is also the simplest. As you focus on being God's friend, others will naturally be drawn to you. Because God's in control, you probably won't attract a person you would previously have chosen, but someone far better instead.

Give yourself time to lay the groundwork for such a friendship. Be patient as celibacy allows you to heal physically, emotionally, and spiritually. Let your sexual restraint have time to build character. After a while, you'll begin to appreciate your true value, and you'll raise your expectations about the way others may treat you. Celibacy will also teach you that building true intimacy through communication is a far better relational foundation than its counterfeit, sex.

The closer you draw to God, the more you'll grow—mentally, emotionally, socially, and spiritually. You'll become a magnet for others who share your passion for God. People will be drawn to your strength of character, quiet confidence, and godly wisdom. It's a simple yet brilliant plan. As God makes you more like Him, you become a perfect match for the one He has made just for you.

Practiced Intimacy

Remember my definition of insanity in the last chapter? You can't expect to repeat your previous dating methods and produce a different outcome.

Do you want a different outcome? Then I'd like to suggest a different method.

"We practice for divorce in our culture," Michael Baggett, singles pastor at Bayside Church in Granite Bay, California, said to me as I met with him to discuss this topic.

"How so?" I asked.

"We start dating, get to know each other, and then we break up," he said. "Repeating that over and over in relationships before marriage makes it common practice. Breaking up after marriage is not that different for us, it's just more complicated."

Dr. Raunikar agrees. He suggests, "If you do a lot of dating, you will do a lot of breaking up. The formula for dating is 'breaking up minus one'—you break up with everyone you date, minus the one you marry, *if* you marry. Breaking up not only has a devastating effect on you as a single, but it also has residual effects on your marriage."[6]

As a marriage and family counselor, Dr. Raunikar discovered that both single and married people will use similar excuses when trying to get out of a relationship.

"The excitement is gone."

"The relationship is too demanding."

"Someone better has come along."

"My partner isn't meeting my needs."[7]

As Dr. Raunikar explains, "Dating relationships condition us to break up in times of adversity. When we hit tough times in marriage, we respond the way past experience has taught us—break up and start over."[8]

Does that sound like your experience? If so, do you think it's possible that the dating process could be the reason? As I reflect on my dating experience and that of others, I'm convinced that our failures are largely due to this harmful practice.

How many years have you wasted dating the wrong person? How much needless pain have you endured because of poor choices? If you want a new outcome, then you need a new method. If you want to ensure that your next relationship will be your final one, then you need to change the way you date.

How? It's simple: reorder the steps. Instead of dating and then becoming friends, become friends first and then choose to date (or "court," as some call it).

I've read and studied books on dating, but I first witnessed this process in actual practice with our sons, Chris and Jeff. They're only in their early twenties, but their example has taught me what I wish I'd known a lifetime ago. While they were in high school we encouraged them not to pair up in girlfriend-boyfriend relationships, but to use that time to make long-lasting, positive friendships with many people—girls and guys. Even though they experienced the usual crushes during those years, they resisted tying themselves down to just one girl.

The result? As they matured they began to recognize what they liked in girls, what personality types fit with theirs, and what qualities to look for in the perfect lifetime mate.

After high school they began college still unattached. Focusing on becoming godly men led them to grow spiritually and to serve in ministries in the company of godly young women. They each met a spiritually mature young lady and spent almost a year building close, nonromantic friendships in a group setting. As the couples grew closer, they realized that their feelings had progressed to romance. The couples prayed for God's direction and confirmation and talked about taking their friendships to the next level, becoming "exclusive."

Here's where it gets interesting. Both of our sons came to us and asked our thoughts on these girls, and how we felt about them dating. Chris also approached the girl's parents and asked for their blessing before he began dating their daughter.

What's great about this process? First, it allows a pair of potential marriage partners to become best friends. You can achieve the highest level of intimacy and develop a relationship of trust—two necessary qualities for a great marriage. Also, as you progress into romance, it's with the belief that God has brought you together, possibly for life. In traditional dating, the relationship is often undefined. The partners could have different intentions, but their limited friendship makes the topic unapproachable. I have heard young people say, "We need to have a define-the-relationship talk." But when couples first become friends, much of that work is already complete. You enter into dating clear about each other's expectations.

Disarming the Power Struggle

One day in a senior high girls' class I wrote this quote from Michael Baggett on the board: "The one who loves the least controls the relationship." I asked the girls if they knew what it meant.

I would summarize their collective response like this: "The one who loves the least decides how far the relationship goes, what they do when they're together, how much time they spend together, and what they talk about."

Why? Because the one who loves the most gives up control. In desperation to receive love in return, the one who loves the most becomes vulnerable to the one who loves the least. This creates not only an undefined relationship, but also an unsafe one. The person in control will often abuse his or her power over the other. Maybe you've experienced this kind of relationship.

In contrast, couples who put off romance until their friendship is strong ensure that their love, each for the other, will grow at the same rate. This averts the tendency toward "love control," the need for late-in-the-game define-the-relationship talks, and the heartache of breakup.

Sound possible?

Becoming friends first provides another benefit. While you're growing closer as friends in groups, your family and other friends are watching you. Their observations offer valuable insight. Those who love us the most and have been with us the longest know us best. They can detect whether the relationship is good for us or detrimental. I appreciated our sons asking for our blessing. They wisely determined that if God were leading them to romantic relationships with their women of choice, those in their life who knew them best would confirm it.

I have been praying for our children's spouses for many years. It's exciting to watch God answer my prayers with women who are His perfect matches for them.

Empowering Purity

Dr. Raunikar[9] suggests there are four stages of friendship, which correlate closely with the five levels of intimacy I discussed in chapter 4. They include: Acquaintance, Casual Friendship, Close Friendship, and Intimate Friendship.

As you progress from acquaintance to becoming intimate friends, your level of spiritual and emotional intimacy will grow deeper. Setting emotional boundaries—for example, how intimate you'll be in conversation and how much time you'll spend together—will ensure that you won't move through the four stages too quickly.

And remember, this is all happening without romance. You're establishing a friendship, so the physical involvement should be limited to hugs, preferably from the side.

Once you get to the intimate friendship level, Dr. Raunikar says you will be sharing at the deepest level, divulging your thoughts on marriage to each other. With the blessing of your family and godly friends, this is when the relationship can progress to the dating or courtship stage, then to engagement and marriage. The length of courting and engagement can be shorter than in traditional dating relationships, because you will have invested much relationship-building time becoming best friends. So the courtship and engagement period can focus on pre-engagement counseling and wedding preparations. During the courtship and engagement phases, Dr. Raunikar suggests that physical boundaries may be broadened to include limited kissing and cuddling.

I think this is a great plan with reasonable guidelines. But even this kind of plan, complete with honorable intentions, can fail without one more ingredient. Throughout Scripture, God says that we must depend on each other in order to live the Christian life successfully. The same is true of success in relationships. You can transform good intentions into reality by setting up a system of support and accountability as the foundation of your relationship plan. Whether your support team includes your family, a godly married couple, or your pastor, you are wise to submit willingly to accountability, especially during the later, more intimate stages of your relationship.

I am proud that our sons are building their relationships according to these principles. They and their ladies continue to focus on becoming the men and women God desires. They have built friendships that protect them all from hidden agendas and broken hearts. As they've progressed into romance, they've set safe emotional and physical boundaries. This ensures that their relationships are characterized by value and honor toward each other. And the foundation of their relationships is the godly wisdom and direction they receive from those who hold them accountable.

The result? Actually, it's what I've already shared with you at the beginning of this chapter:

> But the wisdom that comes from heaven is first of all
> pure; then peace-loving, considerate, submissive, full
> of mercy and good fruit, impartial and sincere (James
> 3:17).

If you build your relationship God's way, according to His wisdom, it will be characterized by all the above. Your love for each other will be *pure;* each of you, in thought and action, will desire to keep the other holy. Your friendship will be harmonious and filled with *peace.* Your actions will be *considerate* towards each other. Your humility will allow you to *submit* to each other in love. Your relationship will be full of *mercy* and grace. The *fruit* of your love will be a blessing to each other and to those around you. *Impartiality* will compel you to honor each other above yourself. The *sincerity* of your intentions for the other's good will ensure that you bring out the best in each other.

This is the relationship you'll find between two wise hearts.

This Heart Can Be Yours

When I teach sexual abstinence in high schools, I often ask the students for a list of the qualities they want in a marriage one day. Regardless of their family's faults, teenagers of all ages can accurately describe the essentials of a lifelong marriage.

What would be on your list? Would it include love, honesty, commitment, faithfulness, trust, friendship, fun, great sex, humor, companionship, communication, deep intimacy, honor, respect? If so, then your list is very similar to the lists created by the teenagers I meet—lists that usually fill a white board.

Amazing! These young people know what a great marriage should look like, even if they've never seen one. They themselves want marriages with these qualities, although they're not sure how to achieve them.

Does a marriage like this exceed your expectations? Would it grant everything your heart desires?

I believe your answer is yes, because God is the One who put those desires in you, and He knows how to fulfill them. In fact, the very qualities we desire in a marriage come out of the fruit of godly wisdom in James 3:17. Purity, peace, submission, mercy, and consideration will lead to honesty, love, faithfulness, and trust.

Two kinds of wisdom: God's and yours.

Yours is more familiar to you; you've been trusting in it for as long as you can remember. How is it working for you? Have you tried and failed, tried again and failed again? Has reliance on your wisdom led you into destructive, unfulfilling relationships? As you've discovered, in the end worldly wisdom will betray you. Every time.

Do you want to stop failing at relationships? Would you like your next one to last a lifetime? Simply trying again—following the same method with someone new—isn't the answer.

Allowing God to make *you* new is.

THANKFUL HEART

Commemorating What God Has Done

thankful, adj., 1. conscious of benefit received, expressive of gratitude

thankful heart, n, 1. a heart that is conscious of and extremely grateful for God's blessings

"Commemorate this day, the day you came out of Egypt,
out of the land of slavery, because the
LORD brought you out of it with a mighty hand."

EXODUS 13:3

'm crazy about rings. I have several. Some are precious in value; others are just for fun.

Every night before I go to bed I take off all my rings, except two. One is made out of silver and the other gold, and they never leave my hands.

The gold band signifies the special covenant that my husband made with me on our wedding day. Big meaning is packed into this tiny circle. The gold says that our love is of the highest value to him, something he will always treasure. The circle of the band means that his commitment is for-ever—no matter what happens. Its presence on my finger means that I am his and he is mine. There's no question; I am taken.

After twenty-four years that gold band has made a per-manent indentation around my finger. Even if I take it off, the impression it leaves is a constant reminder. I wear it on my left hand, in close proximity to my heart, to remind me that regardless of his feelings, in spite of any external or internal pressures we face, whatever the cause of this morning's fight, he promises never to renege on his covenant. Seeing that ring on my hand brings me joy, peace, comfort, and security.

Then there's the silver ring. I wear it on my right hand, and it has a heart on it. And in the center of the heart is a tiny gold cross.

This ring is from God. He gave it to me to symbolize the covenant He has made with me. It reminds me that He claimed me as His own, redeemed me with His Son's blood, healed my heart, and freed me from bondage.

No, I didn't wake up one day and find it on my finger. I didn't pluck it off a burning bush. But it *was* God's idea. He suggested it one evening as I was reading the passage I've quoted above. God told Moses three times in this one chap-ter that Israel was to commemorate what He had done for them. In verse 16, concerning one of Israel's commemorative rituals, God instructed Moses to tell them, "It will be like a sign on your hand and a symbol on your forehead that the

LORD brought us out of Egypt with his mighty hand."

God loves symbols, so it's no surprise that we do, too. They remind us of significant, life-changing events. A commemorative symbol is a constant reminder of a commitment and the one who made it. God knows that we humans are prone to forgetfulness, especially as time goes on and the vividness of our experience fades. When problems arise, we are also prone to despair, doubting that our experience was real or that God's promises were sincere.

As I read Exodus 13, I sensed God saying that He wanted me to have a symbol of His gift of healing. He wanted me to have confidence that His gift was real and would last forever. Now, when I am tempted by feelings of shame, self-condemnation, or doubt, His ring is a reminder that His healing can never be taken away.

My story, of course, goes beyond healing. My little silver symbol testifies to God's astonishing grace, forgiveness, redemption, renewal, and revival. I was broken, and He put me back together. I was bleeding, and He bound my wounds. I was drowning, and He rescued me. I was blind, and He gave me sight. I was emotionally and spiritually dead, and He renewed and revived me. I was wandering off the path, and He brought me back. I felt used up, old, discarded; He restored my youth and gave me purpose. I lost my voice; He restored it. I was despondent, and He blessed me with hope.

I offered Him all I had—a tattered collection of dirty rags. And He transformed them into a stunning collection of precious gems that He treasures.

I wear my silver ring on my right hand for two reasons. First, I didn't want this ring to compete for prominence on the same hand as my wedding ring. Second, I'm right-handed, so my right is my strongest hand. Why is that significant? Often in Scripture, God is described as having a "mighty right hand." The ring on my stronger hand reminds me that God's healing in my life has given me power over the enemy. Whenever I feel Satan trying to weaken me by resurrecting my past, this symbol reminds me that I am no longer subject to his power. God has forever defeated sin in my life—sin of the past, present, and future. I am now full to the whole measure of the fullness of Christ (see Ephesians 4:13). All the power of God lives in me. I have access to it anytime, anywhere, and for any reason.

This circular symbol serves one more purpose: It keeps me thankful. I can be feeling depressed or worried about something, and then I'll feel that little ring pressing into my finger. *Ah, yes,* I then remind myself. *God said He is in control of everything. He loves you. He will never leave you. He will always work out His best for you in any situation.*

As I twirl it around, I am reminded that He tells me to cast all my cares on Him. He promises that when I call out to Him, He hears me and helps me in my time of need.

As I twirl, I pray. As I pray, I praise Him and thank Him for all He's done for me. My praise lifts my spirit, my focus, and my problems to God. In return, He renews my hope. He restores my strength. He readjusts my attitude.

It works like a charm—a charm of divine proportions. My circumstance may not change. The problem may still be as big as ever. But my perspective has shifted. I've gone from despair to hope, from self-focus to God-focus, from complaining to gratitude, from weakness to empowerment. This tiny symbol is a reminder that God is always present and that He's in control. He has already done more than my heart could ever imagine. And He promises to do the unimaginable again and again in my life, especially as I surrender everything to Him.

What unimaginably, inconceivably great work has God done in your life recently? Remembering His miracles from the past will give you peace in the present and hope for the future. His wonders are always worth commemorating.

Moses encouraged the Israelites to put a sign on their hand and a symbol on their foreheads, to proclaim to the world what God had done. But commemorative symbols didn't originate in Moses' mind. Or mine. They were God's idea.

Such a symbol honors Him and inspires us. It doesn't have to be elaborate—just something that lifts your heart to heaven.

For me, it's a tiny silver ring.

GETTING TO YES

S o now what?" you may be asking. "Where do I go from here?"

You may have finished reading this book, but your journey has just begun. The purpose of my message is to unlock and uncover a secret burden that you've kept buried away for years. Maybe decades.

Or maybe it's not a past burden, but something very present. My prayer is that once you understand that you can talk about it safely, you'll find the courage to allow God to lead you to the next step.

Unfortunately, this is where many wounded people stop. You've read a great book, learned some valuable lessons that could make a difference in your life, maybe even gained some insight into the reasons for your painful past.

But...

I can hear that three-letter word. That anchor dragging your dreams and good intentions down into the mire of stagnant changelessness. What comes after that word for you?

But it's not the right time.

But I'm too busy.

But it's just too painful to think about.

But there's nothing I can do now anyway; I can't change the past.

But who would I tell? I don't want to rock the boat in my family or marriage.

But I'm too old.

But I'm too young.

God may have forgiven you, but He'll never forgive me.

What reason is your frightened heart giving you?

Regardless of your reason, I'm certain of one thing: The *but* is shouting in your ear. Excuses always do; that's why we feel compelled to listen. They command our attention. They make sense.

They're so *loud.*

But they're not from God. How do I know? Because God speaks in a small, quiet voice—one that's gentle and soft. He's never obnoxious. He doesn't scream to get our attention.

There *is* someone who uses that approach, and he's our enemy. You know of him. His name is Satan, and his primary purpose is to destroy you.

Maybe you feel as though he's already succeeded. If he has convinced you of this, then he's probably also talked you into simply coping with the consequences as best you can and praying that life doesn't get any worse.

Don't believe it! It's a lie. I lost twenty-five of my best years listening to the same "logic."

Another thing of which I'm certain: God has been speaking to you. You've already heard His voice, but until now maybe you've successfully drowned it out. Why is that? As I've grown closer to God, I've found that His requirements for my spiritual growth are often the very things my flesh fights hardest against. In my case, He required that I tell someone my secrets—the very thing I labored twenty-five years to avoid.

If I'd known then what I know now, I wouldn't have waited so long. Or fought so hard.

Possibly you're hearing God's voice, but you don't recognize it. The thoughts He plants in your mind are foreign to you. And since you don't recognize their source, you're hesitant to trust them.

If you think that might be true, connect up with a spiritually mature person who will be honest with you. Sometimes it takes a godly person to point out God's work in our lives.

God has a specific plan just for you. Second Samuel 14:14 says that He "devises ways" that are unique to you, to make you whole and lead you back to Him.

What's the "way" God has tailor-made for you? I can't tell you what it is, but I have a few ideas to get you started.

And because God *does* know His plan for you, He'll respond to your willingness by nudging you along the right path.

Shoring Up the Foundation

Before we deal with a few pointers specific to your sexual healing, let me emphasize three foundational realities that must be in place before God's work can have its maximum impact in your life.

First, do you know Jesus? Have you given Him your life and accepted His payment for your sins? It's been said that God is a gentleman; He won't force His salvation and healing upon someone who refuses Him.

If your answer so far has been no, this is an excellent time to change it to yes. Invite Him to transform your life as He has mine. Turn back to chapter 8, and read again the portion where I've explained how you can give Him your life and receive His forgiveness.

Second, if you've trusted Christ as your Savior, how often do you spend time with God, reading your Bible and praying? Giving your heart to Jesus is a good start, but often we don't give Him much of our attention. The way to get to know God is essentially the same the way we get to know a friend or a spouse—you spend time with Him.

I have a set time and a specific place that I save just for my meetings with God every day. This habit started out as a discipline I had to work at. But it has now become my favorite part of the day.

Third, do you have a church family? God has made clear the necessity of belonging to a family of believers. The local church is where we're encouraged, built up, sharpened, strengthened, and loved. We will not reach full spiritual maturity without the body of Christ. That's probably why Satan hates it so much and does his best to keep us from it.

Attending Sunday service is a great start. But it's not enough. To get the full benefit, we need a venue during the week that allows us to study and apply what we learn on Sundays, such as a small group Bible study or a place to serve.

These three foundations—salvation, time with God, and a church family—put us physically, mentally, and spiritually into position to learn and grow. And to heal.

Repairing the House

Now, turning to your sexual healing, the most important step you need to take is to seek godly counsel. Christian counseling can be a positive choice for any of the struggles we've discussed in this book. Counselors can often decipher the root of our struggle and offer a beneficial course to take.

Or spend time with a wise, godly person whom you like and trust. Either way, God uses others to help us see realities about ourselves that we can't see by ourselves. And He places people in our lives to support us along our healing journey.

If you've been victimized sexually, whether through rape or sexual abuse, Christian counseling is a must. Also, inquire about a Christian recovery group for sexual victims. My experience and research leads me to recommend employing both counseling and a support group simultaneously.

A great resource while you're receiving this help is *The Wounded Heart*[1] by Dr. Dan Allender. His companion workbook, which has the same title, is a great addition.

If you're struggling with sexual or pornography addiction, or homosexuality, I encourage you to ask your church leaders or a Christian counselor to recommend local Christian recovery groups or Christian rehabilitation organizations. A Bible study I would suggest is *Celebrate Recovery*[2] by John Baker and Rick Warren, a four-part series that addresses these kinds of issues. (The series also deals with substance abuse.)

If you've had an abortion, I highly recommend joining a recovery/support group at a church or faith-based Pregnancy Resource Center (PRC) in your community. I went through a study called *Forgiven and Set Free*[3] by Linda Cochrane, led by other postabortive women at the PRC where I volunteer. Working through it in a group is preferable to doing it on your own. But you'll still find it worthwhile if your only option is to complete the study alone. (The men's version is called *Healing a Father's Heart: A Post-Abortive Study for Men*[4] by Linda Cochrane and Kathy Jones.)

Another great study by Linda Cochrane is *The Path to Sexual Healing*.[5] Once again, working through it in a group is preferable. It's for those who've experienced sexual trauma, whether from abuse, rape, or promiscuity. For victims of sexual abuse or rape, we require prior counseling before joining our study. The reason is that this study examines the choices we often make following the abuse. Many abuse victims, for various reasons, try to deal with the pain by embarking on lifestyles involving promiscuity, sexual and pornography addiction, and abortion. A victim must heal before he or she can deal effectively with subsequent choices. Only then can the victim understand the reasons for the choices, and address them at their root.

Staying the Course

Remember, healing is a process. Years of abuse, promiscuity, and other struggles can't instantly be reversed. God can do anything He wants, and sometimes He does heal instantly. But for reasons that He understands best, He more often guides each person through a slow and steady process that He knows is best for you as an individual.

I began praying for you long before this book found its way to you.

I'm still praying.

I pray that your heart will be ready to receive the truth. That you will respond not merely by hearing and becoming more knowledgeable, but by trusting God enough to *act* on the truth you've learned.

The next step of your healing journey is up to you. But

have courage, my friend. As you continue this journey, you'll discover something that may surprise you: You're not alone!

There's a world of others who share your struggle. A world full of growing, healing people who've been there, who've experienced freedom from burdens like yours. And because God cares so much, He has positioned them just where you need them—by your side. They're all around you.

But you won't recognize them until, in your heart, you say yes to God.

Please say yes.

Acknowledgments

Thank you, David Kopp, for taking a chance on a brand-new author and being willing to champion this book to your publisher. Your support gives me the courage to keep writing.

Many thanks to the hard work of Brian Smith, my editor who felt the heart of this book and helped make its message strong and clear. You may have spoiled me for future editors, if I am privileged with that honor.

Much gratitude to all the wonderful staff at Multnomah who've made my first experience in the publishing world something positive and awe-inspiring. I've enjoyed every part of it.

Ginny, Vicki, and all my favorite authors from our writers group—thanks for your love, prayers, support, encouragement, and editing. This is for all of us.

Rachel, my second-greatest fan, thank you for seeing what I couldn't, and then challenging me to strive for all that God has for me. You're my pastor, my shopping buddy, and my dear friend. Oh yeah—thanks for the idea!

Tamra, Chris, Jeff, and Brian, my wonderful, patient children. Thank you for enduring frozen dinners and washing your own laundry while I locked myself in the office for several months. But mostly, thanks for loving me in spite of myself. You are the truest human example of Christlike forgiveness and unconditional love.

ACKNOWLEDGMENTS

Eric, you are without a doubt the greatest gift God has given me in this life. Your faith in me is the reason I could persevere. I can't thank you enough.

To every reader who's had the courage to explore the secret places of their heart through this book, thank you for trusting me. I hope my journey has encouraged you to trust God.

STUDY GUIDE

How to Use This Study Guide

Individual use

You've spent years trying to forget your sexual past, but now this book has evoked the old memories. That's a good thing, even if it feels rotten. If you'll use this study guide to work through the book's content, you'll give God the opportunity to work His healing in your life and help you put your past into His hands.

I encourage you to use this study guide as devotional material. Take a few questions each day and prayerfully allow God's truth to permeate into every detail and consequence of your past—even the painful, ugly ones. First Peter 4:1 says, "He who has suffered in his body is done with sin." If you'll courageously endure this emotional pain now, you will reap unimaginable joy later. Every decision I've made to follow God has meant some personal sacrifice or suffering on my part. But God has always rewarded me with something incredible in return. I guarantee He'll do the same for you.

In the event that your memories trigger painful and debilitating emotions, I strongly encourage you to enlist the guidance of a licensed counselor as you walk through this. At the very least choose a trusted person with whom you can talk and pray.

Group Use

God uses other people in our lives to help us grow—especially those who are experiencing issues similar to ours. So discussing these questions in a group setting will be extremely beneficial. Working through them together inspires us to stay focused on God when we're tempted to draw back.

I suggest that your group meet for one to two hours at a time, once a week. A minimum of ten weeks is best, to allow group members to establish bonds that will facilitate the greatest amount of open sharing. When I lead a group like this, we meet for fourteen weeks.

Use the study-guide questions as a springboard for discussion. Choose a facilitator who draws people out and is sensitive to the group's memories and emotions.

Establish ground rules up front. The ones we use are:

Confidentiality—an absolute necessity.

Commitment to meet together regularly and to come with questions completed. Attendance is necessary for everyone's growth.

Freedom to allow feelings and emotions to emerge openly without judgment or problem solving from others in the group. To suggest that someone "shouldn't feel this way" negates their feelings. You can affirm the way a person feels, no matter whether you believe they are right or wrong.

Participation by everyone. Be sensitive to those who dominate and those who hesitate in sharing. Try to foster a balance between the voices of all present.

Note: Some individuals within the group may not be ready to share their stories. Although I encourage it, it's not necessary. If everyone is uncomfortable sharing their stories, then leave the opportunity open for group members to offer information as they feel led. In a safe, open environment, people will naturally begin to share in time.

If you have decided to tell your stories in a structured format, then I suggest you all share during the same meeting, taking turns. The facilitator should watch the time, allotting each member an equal amount.

Wait until your third meeting before sharing your stories. Experience has taught me that group members feel more comfortable by this point in the group's life.

Use the first week for introductions, sharing general information, and going over the ground rules. During the second meeting, take a look at the "Introduction" questions. And then share your stories during the third meeting. If this is too early for some in your group to share, you may decide to wait one more week. However, I encourage sharing near the beginning of the study to ensure greater unity up front. Knowing that those around us can empathize with our experience allows for greater comfort and ease in developing intimacy early. Each group will be unique, so allow for flexibility.

STUDY GUIDE

Introduction: The Influence of the Invisible

1. There are many books on sex. "But this book is different. We're not going to talk about you having sex, but about *sex having you.*" What do you think this means?

2. The author has stated in the introduction that sexual bonding has many consequences: It can propel us into promiscuous lifestyles; it can alter our view of ourselves, others, and sex; it can inhibit our ability to form healthy lifetime relationships; it can increase the incidence of divorce; and it can lead to sexual addiction and dysfunction. Do you agree? Why or why not?

3. What "sexual residue" have you acquired through your past experiences?

4. How has this sexual residue impacted you, both in the past and in the present?

5. What do you hope God will do as you surrender your past to Him?

6. Take some time and fill out the first "Symptom Checklist" in the appendix. Fill in the "Past" and "Present" columns. (After you've worked through the entire book and all the lessons in this study guide, repeat the exercise by completing the second "Symptom Checklist.")

Chapter 1: Diary of a Bonded Heart

1. Everyone has a story. What's yours? Below is a list
    of questions to help you get started. Write out your
    story in as much detail as God leads you to do.
    Ask God what He wants you to remember. Trust
    that He will reveal exactly what He wants you to
    see, at the pace that is right for you. You might
    also remember more over the coming weeks.

- What is your first memory of being exposed to
  sex? Describe the circumstances surrounding that
  memory—when, where, how, by whom, and
  how old you were.
- When did you have sex the first time? With
  whom, where, when? What significant circumstances surrounded it?
- How did that first experience impact the next
  choices you made about sex in your life? Write
  down all the sexual experiences and partners
  you can remember.
- What are some of the consequences of each
  sexual experience—physically, emotionally,
  and spiritually?

2. Look back at the questions in the "Introduction"
    lesson above. As you write your story, ask God to
    show you how your sexual experiences are still
    impacting you today.

Note: If you are studying this book in a group setting, wait
until week three to share your stories. See the instructions for
"Group Use" in the introduction to this study guide.

Chapter 2: Recognizing the Sexually Bonded Heart

1. Have you ever thought of sex as being *holy*? After looking at the Scriptures from this chapter, how has your view of sex changed?

2. First Thessalonians 4:6 warns that misusing others sexually wrongs or defrauds them. Describe the wrong or fraud that occurs. How have you been wronged by sex? How have you wronged someone else?

3. Sexual bonding makes two people feel closer than they really are and leads them to initiate sex sooner in subsequent relationships. How have you experienced this in your relationships?

4. In the paper heart demonstration, two hearts were stapled together but only one was torn apart. Can you describe what was torn apart in your broken relationships? How did the resulting emotions impact your next relationship?

5. If you had sex with your present spouse before you were married, how is that impacting your marriage today? Do you lack desire for sexual intimacy? Do you feel disconnected emotionally? Do you experience feelings of guilt or regret associated with your premarital relationship? Anything else?

6. We see in 2 Chronicles 7:14 that when we turn to God, He will forgive us and heal us. What "land" do you want God to heal in your life?

Chapter 3: Understanding the Sexually Bonded Heart

1. Many people find that after they discover the chemistry of sexual bonding, they are able to put a name to what they experienced. How does this information about chemicals and hormones help you understand your current struggles? Describe the connections you see.

2. Realizing that we have decreased our capacity to produce bonding hormones in future relationships can be very discouraging. In Joel 2:25, God says, "I will repay you for the years the locusts have eaten." How does this verse give you hope that God can restore what has been robbed from you? Specifically, what do you want God to restore in your life? Ask Him.

3. Bonding to pornography is common in our culture. If this has happened to you, you are not alone. Allowed to continue, it could lead to destructive behaviors and relationships. In addition to breaking sexual bonds, you will need to take other steps towards healing from this addiction. What is God asking you to do about it?

4. Begin to write your sexual history list. Ask God to remind you of everyone you've had sex with or been involved with in sexually arousing situations. It could include sexually abusive relationships, homosexual relationships, pornographic images, one-night stands, long-term relationships, and even your spouse if you had sex with him or her before

marriage. Write down as much as you'd like about each situation or relationship. Try to identify your emotions during the relationship and after it ended. Take undistracted time to do this. You may need several sessions with God to complete your list.

I know this is very painful. The good news is that you're sharing this secret with God first. There isn't a better person to begin with. In doing so, you'll experience the truest form of intimacy with One who hears your heart and offers you the most amazing grace, mercy, love, and forgiveness. In exchange for your broken heart, God will give you strength and courage.

I want you to anticipate various emotions as you go through this exercise. You may feel anger, sadness, depression, or regret before you experience relief. The exercise may evoke memories of which you are presently unaware. Take comfort—this is normal. Grieving for what was lost and what you've given away is not only natural but necessary, so that you can be released from your invisible bonds. After you have worked through a season of grief, healing will result.

Are you ready to start your list? Let's begin.

Chapter 4: The Heart's Cry for Intimacy

1. As you read about the five levels of emotional intimacy, identify the level at which you began having sex in your relationships. Did you find, as Dr. Joy says, that with each partner you began to initiate sex sooner?

2. Misusing sexual intimacy can impair our ability to experience *true* intimacy. If you're in a relationship now, what is your level of intimacy? Your partner's? If you're not in a romantic relationship, is there anyone among your friends or family with whom you communicate at the highest level?

3. Roger Hillerstrom says that when we begin sex in a relationship, we stall at that relational stage. Do you believe this? Why or why not?

4. As you answered the questions in chapter 4 regarding sexual wounding, what has God revealed to you about your past experiences?

5. After reading about the debilitating lies in the author's experience, what lies can you identify in your thinking? They may be different than those described in this chapter.

6. Take time to read through the Song of Songs in the Bible. Read it through at least five times in five separate sittings. (Leave some time between, to let it soak in.) Write down everything that the Holy Spirit shows you. Ask Him to replace the lies you've learned with His truth.

Chapter 5: The Heart's Cry for Healing

1. Jesus offers us unconditional forgiveness according to 1 John 1:9. Why is it that even when we *know* we are forgiven, we don't *feel* forgiven?

2. James 5:16 says that when we confess our sins to others we are healed. How does that happen? Why would God make this a necessary step in our healing?

3. What is the difference between good pain and bad pain? Describe the role that bad pain has played in keeping you from experiencing healing in your life. What good pain is God calling you to walk through right now?

4. "The greatest impact of sexual sin is relational. What a shrewd plan. What better way to keep people from drawing closer to God than to keep them from trusting people? And if I can't trust you, whom I see, then I most certainly can't trust a God that I can't see." How has sexual damage kept you from healthy human relationships? From a relationship with God?

Chapter 6: New Heart

1. Step one is *surrender*. This is easier said than done. What does surrender mean to you? Are you at the point of total surrender to God? Why or why not? If not, what is keeping you from surrendering everything to God? Pray and ask Him.

2. Step two is *true repentance*, or seeing our sin God's way. Worldly sorrow falls short of true repentance, but it is often our motive for confession. We want relief from sin's ramifications, but not from the sin itself. Godly sorrow results when we see how our sin has affected others, and it

leads to true repentance. Reflect on your sorrow. Is it for you, or is it for others? Ask God to break your pride and expose the true nature of your sin.

3. Step three is examining *the root of our sin*. As you've surrendered everything to God, what has He shown you about your sin? Who has been hurt the most because of your sin? How has a hardened heart towards God impacted your choices? How has it impacted your life?

4. Step four is *obedience*. We will never truly experience God until we obey Him. Growth is circular. When I obey God, I experience Him, which leads me to trust Him and love Him. I am then compelled to surrender more of myself to Him. As I do that, He reveals more areas for obedience, in order to experience more of Him…and so on. If you're stuck spiritually—dealing with the same issues over and over—what are you *not* doing that God is asking you to *do*? What are you *doing* that God is asking you *not* to do?

5. In chapter 3 I asked you to start writing your sexual history list. It's time to pray through this list to begin breaking sexual bonds. Take it slow. Wait on God. Let Him reveal whatever you need to see in order to experience complete healing from each name or incident. Don't be alarmed if it's painful. Walking through the good pain will eradicate the bad pain. Embrace it with open arms. Feel your tears wash you clean. Remember, you're not alone. The One who has gone before you in suffering is also right beside you.

Chapter 7: Virgin Heart

1. Have you prayed through your list yet? How are you feeling? What has God revealed to you in this exercise?

2. Why do you think God compares freedom with youth? How has your past made you feel old?

3. The author describes a heart in bondage as one that "expends all of its energy trying to redeem, justify, hide, and forget the past." Does this describe your experience? If so, how have you gone about trying to redeem, justify, hide, and forget your past?

4. God compares a free person to a calf leaping out of a stall. Have you begun to do some leaping yet? What has God released you from?

5. Malachi 4:2 says that before the calf can leap he has to leave the stall. God has opened the barn door for you. He's offering freedom. But you must get up and go out the door. Have you left the barn yet? If not, what is keeping you from going through the door to freedom?

6. Read again the last three paragraphs of chapter 7. God wants you to experience His transforming, healing power. Meditate on the verses listed in those paragraphs. Does one stand out for you? What is God promising you personally through one or more of these verses?

Chapter 8: Abandoned Heart

1. Do you live as though life is all about relationships? What has your life been about?

2. Have you gone after things that have fueled discontentment? What are they?

3. As you read through the contrasts between proud people and broken people, what stood out to you? Which side do you live on most of the time?

4. Why does Dr. Smalley say we need conflict in order to move to the highest levels of intimacy? What scares you the most about conflict? How can you embrace conflict and honor each other at the same time in your marriage or present romantic relationship?

5. If your marriage or present romantic relationship began with an intimacy handicap, what was it? How is this impacting your ability to communicate now at the highest level of intimacy?

6. Are you hanging on to past lovers emotionally? Physically? Through mementos? Mentally? You may not recognize how they're damaging your marriage or present relationship until you give them up. Are you ready to let them go? Why or why not?

7. A definition of insanity is "doing the same thing over and over, expecting a different result." What ineffective methods are you using to avoid or replace true intimacy with your spouse? How can

you begin to trust God with your intimacy, rather than trusting a counterfeit?

8. What is your level of intimacy with God? What would you like it to be?

Chapter 9: Wise Heart

1. Did you know there were two kinds of wisdom? Which one rules you—godly wisdom or earthly wisdom? To answer, consider the fruit of your life. What kinds of results has your wisdom achieved?

2. Dr. Joy says that the first thing we need in order to begin healing is *time*. Time between relationships allows us to recharge emotionally and heal. If you're between relationships right now, how will giving yourself time help you heal? In what areas do you need healing?

3. After reading this far in the book, list the reasons God gives for saving sex for marriage.

4. The second thing Dr. Joy says we need is *people*. How will nonromantic friendships help you heal? How will nonromantic relationships help you learn to appropriately build true intimacy?

5. "As God makes you more like Him, you become a perfect match for the one He has made just for you." How does your relationship with God prepare you for marriage? How does loving God make you attractive to others?

6. What's your opinion of traditional dating? How has it worked for you? Do you agree that "dating teaches us to break up?" Why or why not?

7. How do you feel about Dr. Raunikar's plan for dating? From what you've experienced in dating, does this plan seem feasible? Why or why not?

8. "Do you want to stop failing at relationships? Would you like your next one to last a lifetime? Simply trying again—following the same method with someone new—isn't the answer. Allowing God to make *you* new is." How do you feel about this statement? How does God want to make you new?

Chapter 10: Thankful Heart

1. How important are symbols to you? Have you ever used a symbol to remind you of something God has done for you?

2. Why does God place great value on symbols?

3. Symbols make the event "real." They help remind us of what God has done, and they keep us thankful, humble, and dependant on God. Why are we prone to forget what God has done for us in the past?

4. What is God urging you to commemorate?

5. What do you want your symbol to remind you of?

6. How can your symbol keep your relationship with God alive and growing?

Conclusion: Getting to Yes

1. As you've read this book, God has pinpointed something that He wants you to address. Is it something in the past, in the present, or both? Write it down.

2. Finish this statement if it applies. "I want to deal with _____ but _____." If you used to have a "but," but you don't now, what has changed?

3. Which of the three foundational elements do you need to put in place in your life? Knowing Jesus as your personal Savior? Spending time with God in prayer and Bible reading? Attending a church body on a regular basis and becoming involved in other church activities? What's your plan to make it happen?

4. Remember, without a plan even the best intentions will fail. Pray first, then write out a plan to make your next step a reality. What does God want you to do next? Call a counselor? Join a Bible study or support group?

5. Ask God to bring names to mind of people who can help you on this journey. You need their support, prayer, and accountability. God has not designed you to succeed alone. If you're tempted to do so, surrender that to Him. Then pick up the phone.

List your support team here:

Name   Phone Number

6. Next, ask God to show you what your particular coping mechanism is. It could be alcohol, legal or illegal drugs, physical or emotional affairs, or escaping into fantasy. It could also include acceptable activities that you carry to excess, such as overeating, shopping, e-mailing, Internet browsing, talking on the phone, reading, watching TV, or playing computer games. Less obvious forms include retreating from people, emotionally and physically.

Once you've identified your coping strategies, plan what you will do instead. Use the chart below to help you.

When we use coping mechanisms during the healing process, we may numb the pain, but we also slow our healing and growth. If we can't feel the pain, we can easily deny that it exists or that it is impacting us negatively. Give *God* the chance to comfort you in your pain, rather than comforting yourself with ineffective coping strategies. After all, He is the Master.

What are my coping mechanisms?	What's my trigger? What situation or emotion do I want to avoid or deny?	What time of day is worse? What place? Which people?	What will I do instead? (Ideas: Go for a walk, pray with a friend, read my Bible.)

7. Last but not least, give yourself some grace. God does. It's not going to get better overnight. This isn't a contest. And there's no deadline. God is always at work in you, even when you can't feel it. So rest in Him, and let Him do His job. Your job is to say yes; He'll do the rest. Remember, *God is on your side*.

APPENDIX

SYMPTOM CHECKLIST [1]

Date: _____

Using the following guide, please evaluate the emotional, behavioral, and physical responses you have experienced that may be related to your past and present sexual damage.

0 = Not currently experiencing 1= Mild 2 = Moderate 3 = Extreme

SYMPTOM	PAST	PRESENT
Have difficulty expressing yourself sexually		
Avoid times of emotional and/or sexual intimacy		
Anxiety/panic/nervous tension		
Feeling numb (esp. during sex)		
Grief/loss/sorrow/sadness		
Regret/guilt/shame		
Loneliness/isolation/difficulty making friends		
Feeling "branded"—as if other people can tell		
Alienation/feeling different from other people		
Depression/hopelessness		
Have a general mistrust of men or women		
Inability to trust myself or my decisions/self-doubt		
Anger/rage		
Feelings of having been victimized		
Feel powerless to assert/protect yourself against sexual harm		
Fear of punishment		
Dreams/nightmares/difficulty sleeping		
Fear or discomfort with sex or with sexuality		
Seasons or cycles of depression/sickness or accident prone		

SYMPTOM	PAST	PRESENT
Flashbacks or hallucinations related to past experiences		
Difficulty concentrating		
Secrecy/difficulty telling others about past		
Difficulty forgetting and/or difficulty remembering past sexual incidents		
Feeling "crazy"		
Crying too much or too easily/inability to cry		
Difficulty bonding with or overprotective of children		
Eat too much or too little		
Increased drug or alcohol use/addiction		
Need to use alcohol/drugs to engage/enjoy sex		
Suicidal thoughts/attempts		
Fatigue/tiredness		
Marital difficulties/marital stress		
Need to be in control		
Promiscuity (many sexual partners)		
Feel unworthy of being loved/cared for		
Struggle with feelings of lust		
Tempted with sexual perversions		
Have self-punishing behaviors		
Struggle with desiring/enjoying sex with your spouse		
Need to fantasize or use pornography to be sexually aroused		
Lowered self-worth/inferiority		

SYMPTOM CHECKLIST [2]

Date: _____

Using the following guide, please evaluate the emotional, behavioral, and physical responses you have experienced that may be related to your past and present sexual damage.

0 = Not currently experiencing 1= Mild 2 = Moderate 3 = Extreme

SYMPTOM	AFTER STUDY
Have difficulty expressing yourself sexually	
Avoid times of emotional and/or sexual intimacy	
Anxiety/panic/nervous tension	
Feeling numb (esp. during sex)	
Grief/loss/sorrow/sadness	
Regret/guilt/shame	
Loneliness/isolation/difficulty making friends	
Feeling "branded"—as if other people can tell	
Alienation/feeling different from other people	
Depression/hopelessness	
Have a general mistrust of men or women	
Inability to trust myself or my decisions/self-doubt	
Anger/rage	
Feelings of having been victimized	
Feel powerless to assert/protect yourself against sexual harm	
Fear of punishment	
Dreams/nightmares/difficulty sleeping	
Fear or discomfort with sex or with sexuality	
Seasons or cycles of depression/sickness or accident prone	

SYMPTOM	AFTER STUDY
Flashbacks or hallucinations related to past experiences	
Difficulty concentrating	
Secrecy/difficulty telling others about past	
Difficulty forgetting and/or difficulty remembering past sexual incidents	
Feeling "crazy"	
Crying too much or too easily/inability to cry	
Difficulty bonding with or overprotective of children	
Eat too much or too little	
Increased drug or alcohol use/addiction	
Need to use alcohol/drugs to engage/enjoy sex	
Suicidal thoughts/attempts	
Fatigue/tiredness	
Marital difficulties/marital stress	
Need to be in control	
Promiscuity (many sexual partners)	
Feel unworthy of being loved/cared for	
Struggle with feelings of lust	
Tempted with sexual perversions	
Have self-punishing behaviors	
Struggle with desiring/enjoying sex with your spouse	
Need to fantasize or use pornography to be sexually aroused	
Lowered self-worth/inferiority	

Introduction

1. Michael R. Pergamit, Lynn Huang, Julie Lane, "Long-term Impact of Adolescent Risky Behaviors and Family Environment," National Opinion Research Center, University of Chicago, August 2001. Executive Summary Page.

Chapter 2

1. Randy C. Alcorn, *Restoring Sexual Sanity* (Ft. Lauderdale, FL: Coral Ridge Ministries, 2000), 120.
2. Gallup Poll, August 6–10, 1996. 1,025 phone interviews.
3. Donald M. Joy, *Re-Bonding: Preventing and Restoring Damaged Relationships,* 2nd ed. (Nappanee, IN: Evangel Publishing House, 1996), 52.

Chapter 3

1. Douglas Weiss, *Good Enough to Wait: Teen Sex Talk* (Fort Worth, TX: Discovery Press). http://www.sexaddict.com.
2. Judith Reisman, "Biologically Arousing Sexual Imagery as Psychopharmacological 'Toxic Media,' 'Harmful to Minors,' Overriding Left Hemisphere Cognition, Subverting Informed Consent and Free Speech," 1993, 1996. Grant for the Ontario Human Rights Commission, Ontario, Canada on *Pornography, Neurochemical Effects on Women.* See also Reisman, *Kinsey, Crimes and Consequences* (Louisville, KY: IME, 1998, 2000, 2003). Chapter

Eight as quoted in No. 03-218, *In the Supreme Court of the United States, John Ashcroft, Attorney General of the United States, Petitioner, vs. American Civil Liberties Union, Et. Al., Respondents, on Writ of Certiorari to the United States Court of Appeals for the Third Circuit* (following remand) page 6. http://www.findlaw.com.

3. Eric J. Keroack and John R. Diggs Jr., "Bonding Imperative" (Sioux Falls, SD: Abstinence Clearinghouse, 2002), 1–3. Article quoted in medical archives of the Abstinence Clearinghouse. http://www.abstinence.net.

4. Dawn McCoy, "Together, Again," *Canadian Living Magazine*, May 2004, 93.

Chapter 4

1. Joy, 52.

2. Robert E. Rector et al, "The Harmful Effects of Early Sexual Activity and Multiple Sexual Partners Among Women: A Book of Charts" (Washington, DC: Heritage Foundation). http://www.heritage.org. This study is based on the National Survey of Family Growth, a survey fielded in 1995 to a nationally representative sample of ten thousand women between 15–44. Sponsored by the Centers for Disease Control and the U.S. Department of Health and Human Services, June 23, 2003, 1.

3. "Divorce and Marriage Rate in the U.S. 1889–1998 (Per 1,000 Population)," National Center for Health Statistics, U.S. Department of Health and Human Services, chart.

4. P. Roger Hillerstrom and Karlyn Hillerstrom, *The Intimacy Cover-Up: Uncovering the Difference Between Love and Sex* (Grand Rapids, MI: Kregel Publications, 2004), 29–31.

5. Ibid., 28.
6. Ibid., 32.
7. P. Roger Hillerstrom, phone interview, October 4, 2005.
8. Linda Cochrane, *The Path to Sexual Healing* (Grand Rapids, MI: Baker Books, 2000), 26, 27, 39, 40.
9. Ibid., 61.

Chapter 5

1. Henry Cloud and. John Townsend, *How People Grow* (Grand Rapids, MI: Zondervan, 2001), 215.
2. Beth Moore, *When Godly People Do Ungodly Things* (Nashville, TN: LifeWay Press, 2003), 20.
3. Dan B. Allender, *The Wounded Heart: Hope for Adult Victims of Childhood Sexual Abuse* (Colorado Springs, CO: NavPress, 1995), 13, 15.

Chapter 6

1. Henry Cloud and John Townsend, 171–73.
2. Beth Moore, 83.
3. Handout adapted from Kathy Edwards, *Breaking Sexual Soul Ties* (Portland, OR: Pregnancy Resource Centers of Greater Portland).

Chapter 8

1. Craig Wilson, "Wealth Isn't Always What It's Stacked Up to Be," *Sacramento Bee*, 28 December 2004. Section E.
2. Rick Warren, *The Purpose Driven Life* (Grand Rapids, MI: Zondervan, 2002), 17.
3. Adapted from Nancy Leigh DeMoss, *Brokenness: The Heart God Revives* (Buchanan, MI: Life Action Ministries).
4. Gary Smalley, *Secrets to Lasting Love: Uncovering the*

NOTES

Keys to Life-long Intimacy (New York: Simon and Schuster, 2000), 95.

5. P. Roger Hillerstrom and Karlyn Hillerstrom, *The Intimacy Cover-Up*, 28.

6. John C. Maxwell, *Today Matters* (New York: Warner Faith, 2004), 99.

7. P. Roger Hillerstrom, *Intimate Deception* (Portland, OR: Multnomah Press, 1989), n.p.

8. "Husband Resents Wife's Male Friends," Dear Abby, *Sacramento Bee*, 12 January 2005.

9. Ibid.

Chapter 9

1. Joy, *Re-Bonding*, 94.

2. Rick Stedman, *Your Single Treasure* (Chicago: Moody Press, 1993, 2000), 141.

3. Joy, *Re-Bonding*, 94.

4. Don Raunikar, *Choosing God's Best: Wisdom for Lifelong Romance* (Sisters, OR: Multnomah Publishers, 1998), 13.

5. Ibid., 92.

6. Ibid., 51.

7. Ibid.

8. Ibid., 51–52.

9. Ibid., 133.

Conclusion:

1. Dan Allender, *The Wounded Heart: Hope for Adult Victims of Childhood Sexual Abuse* (Colorado Springs, CO: NavPress, 1995).

2. John Baker and Rick Warren, *Celebrate Recovery* (Grand Rapids, MI: Zondervan, 1998).

3. Linda Cochrane, *Forgiven and Set Free: A Post-Abortion Bible Study for Women* (Grand Rapids, MI: Baker Books,1986, 1991, 1996).

1

4. Linda Cochrane and Kathy Jones, *Healing a Father's Heart: A Post-Abortion Bible Study for Men* (Grand Rapids, MI: Baker Books, 1993, 1996).
5. Linda Cochrane, *The Path to Sexual Healing.*

Appendix

1. Symptom Checklist adapted from the handout, "Post Abortion Stress Symptom Checklist" (Portland, OR: Pregnancy Resource Centers of Greater Portland).

NOTESNOTES